THE GREAT
HISPANIC HERITAGE

Jennifer Lopez

D1530453

THE GREAT HISPANIC HERITAGE

THE GREAT
HISPANIC HERITAGE

Jennifer Lopez

Adam Woog

CHELSEA HOUSE
PUBLISHERS
An imprint of Infobase Publishing

Jennifer Lopez

Chelsea House
An imprint of Infobase Publishing
132 West 31st Street
New York NY 10001

Library of Congress Cataloging-in-Publication Data

Woog, Adam, 1953-
  Jennifer Lopez / Adam Woog.
    p. cm. — (The great Hispanic heritage)
  Includes bibliographical references and index.
  ISBN 978-0-7910-9724-3 (hardcover)
  1. Lopez, Jennifer, 1970—Juvenile literature. 2. Actors—United States—
Biography—Juvenile literature. 3. Singers—United States—Biography—Juvenile
literature. 4. Hispanic American actors—United States—Biography—Juvenile
literature. 5. Hispanic American singers—United States—Biography—Juvenile
literature. I. Title. II. Series.
  PN2287.L634W66 2008
  792.02'8092—dc22
  [B]   2007031663

Text design by Takeshi Takahashi
Composition by EJB Publishing Services
Cover design by Keith Trego and Jooyoung An
Cover printed by Yurchak Printing, Landisville, Pa.
Book printed and bound by Yurchak Printing, Landisville, Pa.
Printed in the United States of America

This book is printed on acid-free paper.

Contents

Introducing J.Lo

"I was always a singer and a dancer, and I always wanted to be an actress," Jennifer Lopez once remarked to a reporter. "For me, it's all just one thing."1

Always is right. Even as a little girl growing up in New York City, Jennifer yearned to perform in front of others. Whenever they could, she and her sisters sang and danced and acted out their favorite scenes from television and the movies. As she grew older, Jennifer remained focused on becoming an entertainer, and she never wavered from that goal. She *always* wanted to be in the spotlight. Singing, dancing, acting—it did not matter which of these she did. Jennifer liked it all.

And so, with remarkable determination and concentration, Jennifer pursued her goal. She focused first on dancing, then acting, then singing *and* acting. She had some hard times along the way, but Jennifer was always buoyed by one of her most notable characteristics: a rock-solid self-confidence. She

Glamorous Jennifer Lopez, multitalented superstar and international celebrity, poses for photographers at the 2006 MTV Video
Music Awards in New York City. The triple-threat actor/singer/
dancer introduced the Video of the Year at the gala festivities.

has always believed in herself and her ability to prevail. "If I could describe myself in a few words," she once said, "'strong' would be one of them. I know what I want, and I'm willing to go after it."[2] She has also commented, "My mom always told me that if you work hard, you can achieve anything. And it's true. It's one of the truest things ever."[3]

Thanks in large part to that determination, and, as much of the world knows, Jennifer achieved her goals, and then some. Today, she is one of the most famous, instantly recognizable performers in the world, as both an actress and a singer. She has become a role model for millions of people around the world, especially women of Latin descent. . . . and she has also been the object of occasional controversy.

A TALENTED PERFORMER

Because of her Puerto Rican heritage, Jennifer is often described as "a talented Latina performer." This is true, of course, and Jennifer is proud of her achievements as such. *PEOPLE en Español* magazine calls her "the most influential Hispanic entertainer in America."[4] The performer herself comments, "I am incredibly proud of my culture and I think I am a woman who is totally defined by my culture. My temperament, my body shape, the way I am is all very much Puerto Rican."[5]

Yet Jennifer has also worked hard to be recognized as a performer whose ethnic background is irrelevant. As a result, her movie career has been varied. Jennifer's roles have included those written specifically for Latinas, such as her role in *Selena,* the movie that made her an international star. She has also acted convincingly in many roles that had nothing to do with her ethnicity, from thrillers (*Out of Sight*) to romantic comedies (*The Wedding Planner*) and dramas (*An Unfinished Life*).

Meanwhile, Jennifer has also created for herself a wildly successful singing career. This aspect of her career has focused on fusing together several styles of music into a blend she calls "Latin soul." The results have been spectacularly success-ful, including the popular smash albums *On the 6* and *J.Lo*. Recently, Jennifer recorded her first album that is completely in Spanish, *Como Ama una Mujer.*

The beginnings of Jennifer's music career had perfect tim-ing. In the 1990s and early 2000s, she rode the crest of a surge of enthusiasm in America for Latin-based popular music. During this same period, several other singers also came to prominence, including Christina Aguilera, Ricky Martin, and Marc Anthony. The legendary rock guitarist Carlos Santana also witnessed a stunning upswing in his career.

"JENNY FROM THE BLOCK" MAKES GOOD

By almost any measure, Jennifer's commitment to hard work in both her singing and acting careers has paid off hand-somely. When she received $1 million for *Selena,* she became the first Latina actress to reach that level. With the simultane-ous release of her film *The Wedding Planner* and her album *J.Lo*, Jennifer once again made history. She became the first actress/singer of any ethnicity to have both a film and a music album at the number one spots in the sales charts in the same week. She is now the highest-paid entertainer of Latin descent in history, able to command up to $15 million to star in a motion picture.

Meanwhile, Jennifer has diversified her wealth, branching out into several other businesses besides performing. Today, she heads a sprawling empire that includes film and television production companies, a restaurant, and several popular lines of clothing, perfumes, and shoes.

Jennifer's personal wealth has been estimated at $110 mil-lion. She owns lavish mansions on Long Island (near New York City), in Los Angeles, and on Fisher Island (near Miami). In 2007, *Forbes* magazine, which annually ranks the world's wealthiest people, named her the richest Latina performer in America. The magazine also put her ninth on its overall list of the richest women in entertainment.

One of Jennifer's magnificent homes is in the exclusive residential compound of Fisher Island *(foreground)*, off the southern tip of Miami Beach, Florida. Jennifer also has homes in New York City, Los Angeles, and Brookville, N.Y.

In addition to celebrity and money, Jennifer has received a number of honors. For instance, many of her performances have earned praise from film critics, and among her formal honors is a Golden Globe award nomination for her role in *Selena.*

Of course, there has been the seemingly nonstop praise for her beauty. For years, Jennifer has routinely topped various lists of the world's "sexiest" or "most beautiful" women. All in all, not bad for "Jenny from the block," the New York City kid who just loved to sing and dance and act.

"I'M NOT J.LO"

Yet fame and wealth have come at a price. Privacy, for one thing, has become a hard-won prize for Jennifer. She has lived most of her adult life in the fishbowl of public attention, whether or not she has wanted to. Reporters and fans relentlessly examine even the tiniest details of her life on Web sites devoted to her and in countless newspaper and magazine articles or TV shows.

Indeed, it has seemed at times that the public simply cannot get enough gossip about Jennifer Lopez. At one point, a satirical online magazine, *The Onion*, made fun of this never-ending presence in the media. It ran a mock-serious article headlined, "No JENNIFER LOPEZ NEWS TODAY."[6]

Intimately connected to all this publicity has been the semireal character the press calls "J.Lo." This is the wild persona that formed around her during her years of greatest notoriety. The nickname has stuck with her, even though Jennifer says she dislikes it. To her, it represents a false character: "I'm not J.Lo. She's not a real person. She was just a bit of fun that got really crazy. I've never been anyone but Jennifer."[7]

The actress/singer has commented often about her dismay over the constant scrutiny of her personal life. Nonetheless, her critics point out, she has always had a healthy ego and has rarely shied away from publicity. Her personal behavior has also helped fuel the rumor mill.

In particular, her up-and-down love life has been irresistible catnip to J.Lo watchers. A self-described romantic, Jennifer has been married to or seriously involved with a number of high-profile men. Among these have been rapper/entrepreneur Sean ("P. Diddy") Combs, actor Ben Affleck, and Jennifer's current husband, singer Marc Anthony. Also among her former loves are model/waiter Ojani Noa and dancer Cris Judd, two men best known for once having been "Mr. Jennifer Lopez."

A DIVA?

As both her fans and detractors know, over the years Jennifer has developed a reputation, deserved or not, for being a diva, or a performer who can be difficult to work with, self-centered, or demanding of extra privileges. Stories about her outrageous demands include that she must have luxurious bedsheets of at least 250-thread count in hotels, that she must have five-foot-high fans to blow-dry her hair, and that she must have ridiculously expensive foods, cold Cristal champagne, and pitchers of hot milk at a precise temperature available at all times.

Jennifer strongly denies the reputation, insisting that she is no diva. No matter what happens, Jennifer says, she is always simply trying to be herself. "I'm just being who I am," she insists. "I don't try to be nice. I don't try to be not nice."[8]

In any case, she says that the worst of these stories are not true. Perhaps they are simply exaggerations that stem from Jennifer's perfectionism. She has always had a strong work ethic and demands a lot of herself professionally. In the same manner, she demands a lot from those who work with her.

Recently, Jennifer has made an effort to cut back somewhat on the more glamorous, rumor-creating aspects of her life. "For a girl like me, wearing gorgeous clothes and having all this attention was amazing. It was like being a princess," she reflects. "But it didn't take me long to realize that that sort of fame can be scary. The more the circus builds up around you, the more you start to lose all those intentions that get you there in the first place. I was always about being a good performer and working hard, doing movies,

The hard-working Jennifer opened the 28th Annual American Music Awards in 2001 with an electrifying performance of her hit single, "Love Don't Cost a Thing," from her album *J.Lo*. Her stage theme mimicked a Parisian setting, with a monstrous Eiffel Tower in the background.

making music, but that started to get lost in all that crazy stuff."[9]

Instead of "all that crazy stuff," Jennifer has begun to focus more on other, more fulfilling aspects of life. "I want everything," she asserts. "I want family. I want to do good work. I want love. I want to be comfortable. . . . I want it all."[10]

Although Jennifer Lopez has many years ahead of her, her life has already been remarkable. Yet it began normally, in a close-knit neighborhood in the Bronx, a borough of New York City.

On the 6

The 1970s were hard years for the Bronx. Like other parts of New York City and other large urban areas across the country, it was plagued with a variety of serious problems. These included violent crime, unemployment, drug use, and recurring waves of vandalism and arson.

Many longtime residents abandoned the Bronx during this time. They moved to outlying suburbs to avoid the inner city's worst problems. As a result of this abandonment, many of the borough's once-pleasant neighborhoods suffered serious neglect.

One of those areas was a middle-class neighborhood named Castle Hill. Like Bronx residents in general, the people who lived in Castle Hill have traditionally always been tough-minded, no-nonsense types. The families that stayed there despite the changes in the 1970s had to be strong and resilient to survive. Among them were members of Castle Hill's tightly knit Latino community, David and Guadalupe Lopez and their three daughters.

THE LOPEZ FAMILY

Jennifer Lynn Lopez, usually called "Jen" or "Jenny" when she was little, was the middle child of the Lopez girls. Officially, she was born on July 24, 1970, although some sources give her birth year as 1969. Her sister Leslie was a year older, and her sister Lynda, spelled "Linda" in some sources, was two years younger.

Jennifer's parents had both been born in Ponce, the second largest city in Puerto Rico. Both of them came to New York City as children. Lupe's family emigrated from there when she was only two years old. David's family came when he was just six.

David and Lupe both grew up in New York City, and they did not meet until they were adults. After they married, theirs became a classic story of immigrants to America: a story of people who are determined to work hard, better themselves, and make a good life for their children. Guadalupe became a kindergarten teacher in nearby suburban Westchester County. David worked as a computer specialist for the Guardian Life Insurance Company.

The couple raised their daughters in a modest house on Castle Hill's Blackrock Avenue. The building was typical of those housing the Bronx's densely packed, inner-city residents. Jennifer recalls her home as being hot in the summer and cold in the winter. It was no mansion, but, she says, there was always food on the table.

Compared with other neighborhoods, Castle Hill was a fairly rough part of town. For young Jennifer, however, its crowded inner-city streets were perfectly normal. Castle Hill was simply her home, and she had nothing to compare it to. She comments, "To me it was safe. It was all I knew. My

Jennifer's mother, Guadalupe *(left)*, and sister, Lynda *(right)*, are on hand at the premiere of *An Unfinished Life*, Jennifer's 2005 movie costarring Robert Redford and Morgan Freeman. Lynda, Jennifer's youngest sister, is a television news anchorperson.

mother would send me to the store, and I'd go, when I was like eight-years-old."[11]

A STRONG WORK ETHIC

The Lopez family was close and loving but also strict. David and Lupe always placed a strong emphasis on the importance of hard work, determination, and education as a way to succeed in life. The elder Lopezes always tried to set a good example. They instilled in their daughters a strong work ethic by having one themselves. Jennifer recalls, "My parents . . . raised us to do the right things—go to school, get good grades, try to get into college. It was about trying to have a better life. We weren't allowed to hang out on the streets. Parties—God forbid. I'd beg for weeks to go, then have to be home by 11 P.M., when everybody else was just getting there."[12]

Religious observance was another aspect of this positive role modeling. Jennifer's sister Lynda recalls that their parents always led by example, never missing a day of work and faithfully attending church every week. The Lopezes were Roman Catholic, and Jennifer and her sisters attended Holy Family Elementary, an all-girls school connected to the church the Lopez family attended.

Jenny learned the lessons she was taught. Many observers have pointed out that some of the singer/actress's best characteristics as an adult, including her perfectionism, positive attitude, and her self-confidence and devotion to work, can be directly traced to the example her parents set.

Jennifer herself is quick to acknowledge that her upbringing has made all the difference in her life. In her opinion, most kids in her neighborhood were encouraged to aim high, but not too high. Jennifer and her sisters, however, were encouraged to think more boldly. She remarks, "There's a fear [in the community I grew up in] to dream a little bit more, go a little bit higher. . . . If you're really ambitious, then you'll go to college, maybe be a lawyer. Forget being a doctor—it's way too much school to pay for. [Yet] luckily, with my mom and dad, I really did get the feeling that we could do anything if we worked hard enough."[13]

A PASSION FOR PERFORMING

Jennifer was a spirited but generally well-behaved girl. "I was a good kid," she recalls. "I was always hugging people. I was very close to my grandparents and I listened to my mother and didn't do bad things. I didn't curse and I didn't run around. My mother was very strict."[14]

But Jennifer was also a normal kid, which is to say she was active, curious, energetic, and always busy. "I was never naughty," she recalls, "but I was a tomboy and very athletic. I'd always be running around and playing sports and stuff."[15]

The movie *West Side Story*, winner of 10 Academy Awards, was a huge inspiration to young Jennifer Lopez. In this scene, Latina star Rita Moreno (in lavender) dances with costar George Chakiris. The story is an adaptation of the classic romantic tragedy, Shakespeare's *Romeo and Juliet*.

As much as she enjoyed doing these things, most of Jennifer's energy was always channeled into performing for others. Like their mother, all three Lopez girls liked to sing. The girls also enjoyed acting, especially imitating scenes from their favorite movies and television shows. The sisters would perform whenever they could for their parents, grandparents, other members of their extended family, friends, or neighbors.

In fact, they would perform for anyone who was willing to watch and listen.

All the girls had good singing voices, but early on it became clear that the middle Lopez daughter was the one with the real and lasting passion for performing. It was plain that Jennifer had a powerful desire to be in the spotlight. Guadalupe Lopez says of her daughter, "She always loved to sing, but she was also a born actress. . . . Ever since she was a little girl she was acting, living in her own world."[16]

A POSITIVE ROLE MODEL FOR PERFORMING

Jennifer's parents were happy to nurture her passion for performing. This was especially true of her mother, who

"I GOTTA BE MARIA"

Jennifer was bit by the performing bug early, and she could not understand why it did not affect everyone as it did her. She recalls watching a dance recital when she was about six years old: "The girls were performing for a crowd, and I was too young to be in the show, and I remember being so upset about it. So I turned to my friend, and I said, 'Don't you look at that and want to do it, too?' And she said, 'No.' I was baffled! Like, doesn't everybody want to do that? But it's something that you're born with, I think. Well, that's how it was for me."*

As she grew up, she remained firmly set on becoming an entertainer, specifically, a big star. She says, "I always wanted to sing and dance and be in movies, but when you're little, you don't really understand what the 'rich and famous' part is all about—it's just a catchphrase that means [points at imaginary screen] 'I wanna be doing what they're doing up there.' And ever since I was three that's how I was—I always felt all this drama inside of me."**

loved classic Broadway-style movie musicals and frequently watched them on television with her girls. Jennifer also came to love these movies, and she idolized the great Hollywood female stars of the past. She remembers, "I grew up watching true divas of the cinema like Ava Gardner, Rita Hayworth, Marilyn Monroe. . . . I dreamt about being as glamorous as they were."[17]

Jennifer admired one performer in particular, singer/dancer Rita Moreno. Born in Puerto Rico and raised in New York, Moreno was, at the time, one of the very few prominent Latinos in show business. She was one of the first Latinos (and one of only a handful of performers ever) to win all four major performing awards: a Tony (for theater), an

A major influence on Jennifer was her favorite movie musical, *West Side Story*. This award-winning film was based loosely on the story of *Romeo and Juliet* and set in Jennifer's home territory, a Puerto Rican neighborhood in New York City. Its female stars were Natalie Wood as Maria and Rita Moreno as Anita. Their characters were in sharp contrast to each other, and the two battled for the young Jennifer's affections. She recalls,

"I've seen [*West Side Story*] more than a hundred times and I'd watch right now, if I could. I loved that it was a musical and about Puerto Ricans and that they were living where I lived. I wanted to be Anita because I love to dance and she was Bernardo's girlfriend and he was so hot. But then Maria was the star of the movie. So it was basically like, I gotta be Maria."***

   *   Quoted in David Keeps, "It's Hard to Be Me (But It's Good)." *Marie Claire*, September 2004.

  ** Quoted in Brantley Bardin, "1998 Woman of the Year: Jennifer Lopez." *Details*, December 1998.

***   Ibid.

Emmy (for television), a Grammy (for music), and an Oscar (for film).

Moreno was a very powerful role model for young Jennifer. She was beautiful, an electrifying talent, a woman, and Latina. On top of that, she was Puerto Rican and from New York. Furthermore, her most famous role, for which she won a Best Supporting Actress Oscar, was in *West Side Story*, a musical set in Jennifer's home territory of New York City's Latino community. Jennifer recalls that, since there were no Latinos on TV during her childhood, Rita Moreno was the only performer with whom she identified.

SOAKING UP MUSIC

Lupe Lopez enrolled her daughter in voice and dance lessons when Jennifer was just five. Jennifer continued to take lessons, which included classical ballet and jazz dance at a local Boys and Girls Club, into her teens. She also appeared in locally produced shows, such as musicals that the Boys and Girls Club sponsored. For a time, she also studied traditional Latino dance styles with a distinguished Manhattan-based troupe, Ballet Hispanico.

Meanwhile, Jenny was being exposed to the many varied and vibrant styles of music that were popular among residents of her neighborhood. When she was very young, Jenny mainly heard the styles of music that her parents listened to; Both David and Lupe liked traditional Latino pop styles such as salsa, meringue, and *bachata*. These were the styles that formed the basis for popular dance music and song in Latin America, especially in the Caribbean. Lupe also loved rhythm and blues and other popular dance and vocal music that came from the African-American community. Since the Bronx is home to a variety of ethnic groups, each with its own vivid musical styles, she was able to hear a wide variety of music everywhere she went.

"'RAPPER'S DELIGHT' CHANGED MY LIFE"

Jennifer soaked up all of the music, but one type that hit her especially hard came right from her home in the Bronx. This was rap, which was just beginning to emerge in the late 1970s when Jenny was a preadolescent. Also called hip-hop (the terms have become interchangeable), rap had been mostly underground before that, known primarily to a small segment of the black and Latino communities in the Bronx.

By the time Jenny was old enough to listen to and appreciate music other than what her parents played, rap was just beginning to reach a wider audience. One song in particular, "Rapper's Delight," by the Sugarhill Gang, a Bronx group, became significant to her. "Rapper's Delight" was not the very first rap song, but when it became a hit in 1979, it was the first to be heard by a significantly large audience outside of the New York area. It had a huge impact on young Jenny Lopez.

"'Rapper's Delight' changed my life," she recalls, "but when I came home, my mother would be listening to [salsa stars] Celia Cruz, Tito Puente, [and pop singer] Diana Ross."[18] All of these styles of music appealed to Jenny, and they began to overlap and blend together in her mind. Later in life, she would fuse them together to create her own style, a musical blend she would call "Latin soul."

A FIRST LOVE, A FIGHT, AND A BROKEN NOSE

Of course, listening to music and nurturing her passion for performance were not the only things in Jennifer's life during her grade-school years. Romance, something else that would also become a well-known part of her public persona in years to come, began to make an appearance.

Her first crush was in third grade, on a kid named Charles. Jennifer recalls that Charles had beautiful blue eyes and black hair. She says, "He'd come over to my house every day and my mom would give us sandwiches and milk. I dreamt of marrying him."[19]

Jennifer credits the Sugarhill Gang's hit, "Rapper's Delight," as having a major impact on her musical tastes. The pioneering single sold millions of copies and helped establish hip-hop as a powerful movement in American culture and musical direction. The original group *(shown)*, Wonder Mike, Master Gee, and Big Bank Hank, still tours, as shown here in an MTV Networks Upfront performance in New York City.

Life was not all dreamy romance, however, during her grade school years. Jennifer had a temper, and she got into a few fistfights with other girls when she was young, although she says that the last one was in fourth grade. She recalls, "It was pretty ugly, and although I'm not proud of the event, I did win the fight. Nobody ever messed with me after that, and I graduated from school unscathed."[20]

As she reached her teens, Jennifer's life occasionally had other rough patches. One was a car accident in which she barely escaped serious injury. At 13, Jenny was in the car with her mother when a truck hit them. One of the truck's headlights flew off, smashed through the car's windshield on the passenger side, and landed in the backseat. Fortunately, Jennifer was bending down to tie a shoelace at the moment of impact. If she had been sitting upright, the flying headlight would have struck her directly in the face.

As it happened, Jennifer did suffer a fractured nose in the accident. After it healed, the injury gave her face a distinctive profile, and her nose still looks slightly flat if viewed in a certain way. However, the imperfection does not seem to bother Jennifer. She comments, "People always tell me I look like I was hit with a hammer, but I like my nose. In profile it's good, but if you look straight at me or touch it, you can see the flatness."[21]

HIGH SCHOOL

Jennifer attended another all-girls Catholic school, Preston High School, located near the East River in Throgs Neck, a neighborhood of the Bronx. Unlike her earlier school that had been walking distance from home, Preston was not close by. She had to take a subway and a bus each way to get there.

In most respects, Jennifer's years in high school were uneventful. She was active in drama and took part in school musicals whenever she could. She had a succession of part-time jobs after school, including one in a clothing store. She maintained her interest in athletics, participating in gymnastics, track, softball, and tennis. Only occasionally, she says, did her high spirits get her into trouble with the nuns who taught at Preston High.

Overall, Jennifer says she was neither very well liked nor disliked at Preston. She recalls, "I wasn't the most popular girl in class. I had my friends, but I was comfortable with myself. There's always those most popular girls and I wasn't one of those."[22]

Nonetheless, it was during these years that Jennifer's romantic streak kicked in and she began dating seriously. In particular, when she was 15, she became romantically involved with a boy named David Cruz, whom she remembers as the best-looking guy in the neighborhood. David and Jennifer remained a couple for nearly a decade, despite her parents' efforts to downplay the relationship. She says she was usually able to find ways around her parents' strictness, even if it meant climbing out windows, jumping off roofs, or letting David sneak up.

A FIRST MOVIE ROLE

Jenny's interest in spending time with David did not stop her from continuing to focus on her dance, theater, and voice lessons. She was determined to create a career for herself on Broadway. Jennifer's dreams of public performance were fueled when, still in high school, she won a small part in a movie, *My Little Girl*. This was a low-budget, independent film that was shot in Philadelphia and released in 1987.

Jennifer played a teen from the inner city who is tutored by a rich girl. It was a small role, and the film was not widely seen. Nonetheless, it was a thrill for her to have the chance to act in the same movie as such talented performers as James Earl Jones, Geraldine Page, Peter Gallagher, and Mary Stuart Masterson.

During this period, Jennifer's personal fashion sense continued to develop and change. For a few years, she favored a boyish, hip-hop-influenced look that featured such touches as tight jeans and boots. When Madonna came along in the mid-1980s, however, Jennifer was strongly influenced by her.

She changed her style to reflect the performer's distinctive look. She also emulated Madonna's habit of changing her fashion sense often to create a bold new style. Jennifer remarked that she always admired Madonna's music and sense of style, especially because she changed them often.

"IT WAS A FIGHT FROM THE BEGINNING"

Jennifer graduated from Preston High in 1987, earning only average grades. Actually, despite her parents' urging, Jennifer had never been very interested in academic excellence. Later, when a reporter asked what she had gotten on her SAT tests, Jennifer joked, "Nail polish."[23]

Jennifer's parents had hoped that she would go on to law school and become a lawyer. Yet Jennifer had caught the performing bug in a big way by now, and she was determined to pursue her dream. People in her neighborhood, even her friends, were skeptical. "When I said I wanted to be a performer," Jennifer recalls, "people went, 'Yeah, right.' You don't do that where I come from."[24]

Jennifer has since commented that it was a good thing she did not study law because she would have been a disaster as an attorney. She jokes that she would be in front of the jury singing. Still, she wanted to please her parents, so she agreed to enroll in pre-law classes at Baruch College. Baruch is part of the system of schools that make up the City University of New York in New York City. Yet college was not for her, and Jennifer lasted only one semester at Baruch before she decided to quit school and pursue show business full time.

Having to tell her parents about the decision to quit school was one of the hardest things she has ever done, says Jennifer. They were upset and worried that she was chasing a hopeless dream of becoming an entertainer. Jennifer recalls, "When I told my parents I wasn't going to college and law school—which was aiming really high where I came from, but it was an attainable goal—they thought it was really stupid to go off and be a movie star. No Latinas did that—it was just this stupid . . . idea to my parents and to everybody who knew me. It was a fight from the beginning."[25]

ON HER OWN AND ON THE 6

Jennifer's announcement, and her parents' reaction to it, escalated into a series of heated arguments. Eventually, she left the house on Blackrock Avenue and moved out on her own. It was the first time Jenny had been away from her family.

She lived in a succession of cheap apartments in the Bronx that she shared with friends. She also found a part-time job in a law office, since her parents no longer agreed to support her. The job gave Jennifer just enough money to pay for her living expenses, such as rent and groceries, and for her ongoing lessons in singing, acting, and dancing.

Jennifer also started going to theatrical auditions whenever she could. The auditions, trial performances for entertainers to show off their skills, took place in Manhattan, which is also where many of Jennifer's classes took place. She had a long subway ride on the Number 6 train to get into Manhattan and back home.

This frequent subway ride became a significant part of Jennifer's life, and it would later inspire the title of her first album. To the aspiring performer, the subway commute represented a major turning point in her career. Riding the Number 6, Jennifer later remarked, was a big part of "making the transition from this girl in Castle Hill who could have been a lawyer to dancing, singing and auditioning, letting the artist in me come out."[26]

But recognition for that artistic expression would come later. For the moment, Jennifer was just starting her life as an adult. It would continue to be a struggle for some time to come.

Fly Girl

Life on her own was tough at first for Jennifer, and trying to break into show business was doubly tough. She says she spent a lot of time counting her pennies, and there were many occasions when the aspiring performer was flat broke. For a short time, Jennifer did not even have a place to stay and had to sleep in the studio where she took dance lessons.

Jennifer's main goal at this point was to become a dancer in Broadway musicals. According to her, it actually seemed more likely for her sister Leslie to become a pro, but Leslie did not have the taste for sticking it out. Both sisters started out in musical theater, and Jennifer recalls that Leslie had the better voice and greater chance of making it but that she was less willing to take rejection.

As it turned out, Jennifer's first paying gig of any significance was not on Broadway, but at least it was in the same style. She won a spot as one of the dancers in a five-month tour through Europe of a revue called *Golden Musicals of Broadway.*

In retrospect, Jennifer says that it was a good experience because it gave her an early taste of being on stage. Yet being in a traveling show was also a tough and grueling job. Jennifer was especially frustrated that she was the only member of the troupe who did not get a solo dance spot in which she could shine.

"GREAT, LET'S HIRE HER!"

This job was followed by more satisfying experiences, including a tour of Japan in a show called *Synchronicity* in which she was both a dancer and choreographer. Engagements such as this one, however, were few and far between. For the most part, Jennifer made endless rounds of auditions and got only an occasional gig. Many of these jobs were dull and poorly paid. Most often, she was hired as a background dancer for music videos, which were still a relatively new form of media. She recalls, "I'd dance in a piece-of-garbage rap or pop video for 50 bucks and make the money last a whole month."[27]

Jennifer soon began to benefit from the public's changing tastes in popular music and music videos. Rap had once been an underground trend appreciated by only a few, but now it was entering the mainstream and becoming popular everywhere. In large part, this was due to performers like MC Hammer, whose monster hit "U Can't Touch This" helped make the genre acceptable to a wider audience.

Soon, increased demand required increased supply. As rap became more popular, music video producers scrambled to find background dancers who knew the moves. These were still rare, but Jennifer fit the bill. In fact, Jennifer says, she was doubly in luck because of her Latin heritage. She told a reporter, "Hammer came out with 'U Can't Touch This,' and all the auditions started becoming hip-hop auditions. I was good at it, and they were like, 'Ooh, a light-skinned girl who can do that. Great, let's hire her!'"[28]

IN LIVING COLOR

Among the rap videos she appeared in was "Summertime" by Doug E. Fresh and the Get Fresh Crew. In that video, a close-up of Jennifer's face can be seen in one shot. Gradually, Jennifer became more in demand. Still, it was a struggle until Jennifer caught a break with her first high-profile gig, as a dancer for a new television comedy program called *In Living Color*. Jennifer was rejected twice for the job, but then she auditioned again and won out over some 2,000 other hopefuls who had participated in a nationwide search.

In Living Color, which debuted in 1990, was a comedy sketch show with a strong emphasis on African-American humor. It was a huge success and helped launch the careers of a number of then-unknown comics. Among these were the Wayans brothers, Jim Carrey, and Jamie Foxx.

Jennifer was chosen to be a member of the Fly Girls. This troupe of dancers was hired to perform during short breaks between the comedy sketches and sometimes appear as extras in the sketches. In some ways, it was a great job. For one thing, Jennifer would be making excellent money: more money than her father earned and far more than she had ever made on her own.

On the other hand, taking the new job meant that Jennifer would have to move to Los Angeles, where the show would be taped. The aspiring dancer, Bronx born and bred, did not look forward to this cross-country move. However, the offer was too good to resist.

MOVING TO L.A.

Jennifer says that a big part of her decision was the chance to get out of the dispiriting round of dance auditions in New York. "Once I started working professionally," she recalls, "I realized I couldn't make a living roaming around New York with a big bag on my back, hustling, trying to get a video or a commercial. [Other dancers and I] were struggling, and all our energy went into that struggle, you know?"[29] Jennifer decided to make the move despite her reservations.

In fact, at first Jennifer did hate life in Los Angeles. She missed her family and friends as well as the familiar surroundings of New York. Another reason she was unhappy was that, at least in the beginning, she did not have much fun during the taping of the show. In her opinion, *In Living Color*'s choreographer, Brooklyn-born Rosie Perez, put extra demands on Jennifer, singling her out for harsher treatment than the other Fly Girls.

Yet things soon got better. For one thing, Jennifer was less lonely after her boyfriend, David Cruz, moved to L.A. to keep

FIGHTING FOR WHAT YOU WANT

When Jennifer was struggling to make a living as a dancer in New York, she grew accustomed to going to tough auditions as often as possible, competing against other dancers and hoping that someone would eventually give her a chance. Early on, she realized that it was necessary to be strong.

She once remarked to a reporter, "I have this attitude—and it won't change no matter how big I get—that you have to fight for things you want. You can't expect things to be handed to you on a platter, even if you can fill theaters week in and week out. Because there's always somebody like me ready to kick down the door and steal the job right out from under you."*

According to Jennifer, some people in show business have resented the fact that she was a woman who was so ambitious. She says, "I don't think ambition is a bad thing. But I think sometimes people try to make it sound like it's unattractive to be ambitious and be a woman. But, for me, it's like I had a lot of dreams that I wanted to fulfill, and things that I wanted to go after. And just because I do that, and I have tunnel vision when her company. After that, she settled more easily into her new surroundings. Jennifer was still unhappy with the show and considered quitting, but she ended up staying with it through its full run, from 1990 through 1994.

A big reason for her persistence in staying with the show was that she listened to the advice of Keenan Ivory Wayans, the guiding force behind *In Living Color*. Wayans convinced Jennifer that remaining a cast member would give her valuable experience. At the same time, he told her, she would be paid well and could work on what was now her main goal, her acting career.

Jennifer remained with *In Living Color*, continued to take acting lessons, and furthered her chances for success in other ways. For instance, she took care of her body and health. She

I'm doing it, it doesn't mean that I'm a bad person. If a guy does that, it's like, 'He's great, he's focused.' But when it's a woman, it's a different story. And I just think that's unfair."[**]

Jennifer feels that the kind of childhood she had, and the neighborhood she grew up in, helped a lot in forming her attitude about surviving in show business. She remarks, "I have to say that the kind of upbringing I had, getting beat up a little bit, growing up with all different kinds of different people, is the best upbringing for show business. The people who grew up softer, who don't have what it takes to really survive in this business—that's why you find so many people on drugs [in show business]."[***]

[*]   Quoted in Stephen Rebello, "The Wow." *Movieline*, February 1998.
[**] Quoted in Sean Combs, "Touched by an Angel: Puff Daddy Interviews the Celestial Jennifer Lopez." *Notorious*, October 1999.
[***] Rebello.

Jennifer was a Fly Girl dancer on the FOX Network's smash-hit variety show, *In Living Color.* The show ran for five seasons, from 1990 to 1994, with Jennifer appearing in seasons three and four. The cast included Jim Carrey *(top row, red jacket)* and Jamie Foxx *(seated, wearing black-and-red vest.)*

jogged, worked out, watched her diet, and worked on getting rid of her Bronx accent. She also quickly adopted a philosophical attitude about auditions and missed opportunities. According to her, the important things were showing up at auditions for parts that interested her and forgetting about the times that she was not chosen for the parts.

"THE GIRL JUST HAD IT"

Despite her misgivings, Jennifer's move west proved to be a major step forward for her. It put her in just the right place to move on to bigger and better things. Writer Patricia Duncan notes that the move to L.A. "was probably as important a step as joining the show was, since it got her to Hollywood and put her in a much better position to vie for other roles."[30]

Those roles soon started coming. In part, this was due to the efforts of her new manager, Eric Gold. She had met Gold because he was the coproducer of *In Living Color*. Gold's connections in the entertainment industry helped Jennifer find satisfying work, but he is quick to point out that most of the credit should go to the entertainer herself. Gold says that she had a quality that casting directors responded to when she went to auditions: "There was just an unshakable confidence about Jennifer. No doubt, no fear. The girl just had it."[31]

Her first significant gig after *In Living Color* came along just as the show was winding down in 1994. That was when she appeared as a backup dancer in the video for Janet Jackson's song "That's the Way Love Goes." Jackson was riding high at the time as one of the biggest pop stars in the world, so it was a high-profile job for Jennifer. Jackson was sufficiently impressed to offer Jennifer a full-time engagement as a backup dancer.

Jennifer considered taking it, but before she could make a decision, she was offered an acting job. A respected Hollywood producer, Ralph Farquhar, was developing a new comedy-drama series for television called *South Central*. It centered on the life of a black family in Los Angeles and included in its promising ensemble cast a young Larenz Tate. Since Jennifer wanted to keep her main focus on acting, she accepted the job.

SOUTH CENTRAL, SECOND CHANCES, AND HOTEL MALIBU

Jennifer's character on *South Central* was Lucy, who worked in a food co-op with the character played by the show's lead actress. The part of Lucy was a rarity. At the time, there were almost no Latino roles on television. In fact, according to a study by the National Council of La Raza, Latino characters were less prominent on prime time television in 1994 than they had been in the 1950s, when Cuban-born Desi Arnaz rode high on the ratings as the costar of the nation's top show, *I Love Lucy.*

South Central lasted only one season, and Jennifer's appearances were brief. Nonetheless, appearing on the show was a good move for Jennifer. She stood out as a talented young actress and soon landed another role on a new series. This was a short-lived drama called *Second Chances.* Jennifer was cast as Melinda Lopez, a student who had a stormy relationship with her strict father. *Second Chances* was a high-quality show and might have been a hit, but after one season it fell victim to a double dose of bad luck. The show's star, Connie Sellecca, became pregnant, which limited the amount of time she would be available for taping future shows. Then a major earthquake hit the Los Angeles region, damaging the show's sets beyond repair.

As a result, *Second Chances* was cancelled, although Jennifer's character was not. Her character, and the actress herself, had proved to be so popular with audiences that Melinda Lopez was simply moved to another new series, *Hotel Malibu.* In her new incarnation, Melinda was a bartender-in-training at a luxury hotel. That series also lasted only a single season, but Jennifer's talents as an actress were being noticed increasingly.

Jennifer appeared in 1995's *Mi Familia/My Family* playing the character of Maria Sanchez. Directed by Gregory Nava, the story traces, over three generations, a Mexican family's trials, tribulations, tragedies, and triumphs. Jennifer was nominated for Best Supporting Actress by the Independent Spirit Awards, the premier awards event for the independent film community.

THE FIRST MOVIE ROLES

When she was not taping a show, Jennifer continued to make the rounds of auditions for future roles. She was certain that the right one, the one that would vault her to stardom, would soon come along. As a result, she was now focusing her attention on getting roles in film as well as TV. Her public profile kept rising too. After the demise of *Hotel Malibu*, she played a young nurse in a made-for-television movie, *Nurses on the Line: The Crash of Flight 7*, about an airplane crash in the Mexican jungle. It was not a brilliant movie, but it was a further step up for Jennifer, who had now progressed from a TV series to a TV movie and then to her first film appearances since her small role in *My Little Girl*.

In 1995, she took an even bigger step into feature films, winning a standout role in a well-received independent movie, *Mi Familia/My Family*. This heartfelt saga chronicled three generations of a Mexican-American family. In it, Jennifer played Maria, a nanny in Los Angeles who falls in love with a gardener. Critics and audiences took notice of her vibrant performance. At the same time, many of the people who were involved with the movie's production were impressed with Jennifer's willingness to do whatever was necessary to complete a scene. For example, at one point Jennifer needed to wade into an icy river, fighting her way through the rapids with a baby clutched in her arms. She would not let a stand-in take her place.

Jacob Vargas, who played the gardener Jennifer's character falls in love with, recalls, "She got right into that freezing water every day for three days [as the scene was shot] and came through without ever complaining." Director Gregory Nava, however, recalls the incident a little differently. In Nava's retelling, Jennifer was willing to do the difficult scene over and over simply because she would not risk having anyone else mess it up. Refusing to let a stuntwoman swim in the raging river in her place, she said, "Get her out of there—she's ruining my performance!"[32]

ON THE MONEY TRAIN

Thanks to her performance in *Mi Familia/My Family,* Jennifer was offered a number of higher-profile parts. The first of these was a costarring role in a 1995 comedy-action film, *Money Train.* In this movie, Jennifer plays Grace Santiago, an undercover cop who works in the New York City subway. Her partners on the job, played by Wesley Snipes and Woody Harrelson, are foster brothers, and she becomes romantically involved with both.

Jennifer's role in *Money Train,* for which she was paid $200,000, more than she had ever gotten before, was not race specific. The fact that she was Latina did not matter. The film's director, Joseph Ruben, simply wanted a beautiful, sexy actress who could fuel the chemistry of the story's romantic triangle. Ruben also needed an actress who was physically fit because the role was a demanding one. Furthermore, he needed someone who could play a spirited New Yorker. Jennifer easily fulfilled all of these requirements. To prepare for the role, the actress followed real transit police on the job, learning about their exciting yet dangerous work. Jennifer was especially interested in speaking with female officers because she wanted to learn how they related to their male partners.

As it turned out, Jennifer had some real-life trouble relating to her on-screen partners. Both of Jennifer's costars flirted with her on the set, but she later revealed that Snipes was more serious about it. She commented: "Wesley—even though I had a boyfriend at the time—went full court press. He was flirting with me—you always flirt with your costars, it's harmless—then he just started getting a little more serious. He would invite us all out together and then at the end of the night, he'd drop me off last and try to kiss me. I'd be like, 'Wesley, please, I'm not interested in you like that.' He got really upset about it. His ego was totally bruised. He wouldn't talk to me for two months."[33]

TEACHING *JACK*

Money Train was a respectable hit at the box office, although reviews of it were poor. In fact, a number of critics singled out Jennifer's role as the only good thing about the movie. One person who noticed her appealing performance was director Francis Ford Coppola.

Coppola, famous for his brilliant *Godfather* trilogy and other movies, offered Jennifer her next role, as a schoolteacher in the 1996 comedy-drama *Jack*. She won out over several better-known actresses, including Ashley Judd and Lauren Holly, for the role.

Jack stars Robin Williams as a boy with a rare disease that causes him to physically grow old too fast. Jack is a 10-year-old kid with Williams's powerful adult body. This makes Jennifer's role as his fifth-grade teacher a bittersweet one. Her student is a grown-up in body but not in mind, and it is touching when he develops a schoolboy crush on her. At the same time, the teacher knows that Jack's disease will not let him live to full adulthood.

Despite the film's bittersweet quality, appearing in *Jack* was a pleasant experience for Jennifer. It was a pleasure for her to play a different type of role than she had done earlier. Finally, she says, she was portraying someone who was "not tormented or tough." Also, Jennifer did not have to look far to find someone to help her study for the role of a schoolteacher. She simply called her mother.

Furthermore, she felt very comfortable on the set of *Jack*. The movie was shot on and around Coppola's home, an estate in the winemaking country of California's Napa Valley. The director worked hard to make everyone involved, including Jennifer, feel welcome and at ease during the shoot. He even gave Jennifer's boyfriend, David Cruz, a small, nonspeaking role as her husband in a scene near the end of the film. Jennifer says Coppola was a fine director to work with, always looking for input from his actors. She comments, "Francis is not the type to make you read the script over and over. We did a lot of improv [improvisation] on *Jack*."[34]

"WHAT AM I DOING IN THIS ROOM WITH THESE PEOPLE?"

Jennifer's next movie, also released in 1996, was a thriller called *Blood and Wine*. In this film, she has a supporting but important role as the sexy Cuban-born mistress of a wealthy wine merchant in Miami, Florida. Gabriella, her character, is an immigrant who is desperate to do well in her new home to help her family get ahead. As a result, she becomes involved in a deadly plot, as the wine merchant and a professional safe-cracker conspire to steal a valuable necklace.

In *Blood and Wine* she worked with another gifted director, Bob Rafelson, as well as two screen legends, Jack Nicholson as the wine merchant and Michael Caine as the safecracker. At first, Jennifer was astonished and intimidated to find herself in a production alongside these two film giants. On the first day of rehearsal, the cast gathered around a table to read through the script, and Nicholson sat down next to her. Jennifer recalled, "The director wanted me to sit next to him [Nicholson] because ours was the prominent man-woman relationship in the film. Michael Caine was sitting on the other side, and I looked at one and then the other. Then it was like I had an out-of-body experience! I wondered to myself: 'What am I doing in this room with these people?' It was very scary. But fun."[35]

A NEW LOVE

While this film was shooting, a new chapter in Jennifer's personal life began. For some time, her 10-year-old relationship with David Cruz had been fraying. A major reason for this was that Cruz had never found a comfortable career niche for himself in Los Angeles. He found it particularly hard to accept his lack of progress in the light of Jennifer's growing success. She comments, "He came out here with me and was here with me

Jennifer appears with her first husband, Cuban-born Ojani Noa, at a film premiere in Los Angeles in April 1997, shortly after their marriage in February. The couple met while Noa was working as a waiter in a Miami restaurant. The couple divorced in January 1998.

the whole time when I first started doing television and break-ing into movies. Career-wise, we weren't in the same place. He just didn't know what he wanted to do. But I had a fire under [me], I was so fast. I was like a rocket, he was like a rock."[36]

Adding to their problems, Jennifer says, was the fact that Cruz was uncomfortable when she played intimate love scenes onscreen. She told a reporter that he could be insecure because of these scenes. She would explain that it was her job to make it look as if her costar was the only person in her life, and that it was just acting, but this was hard for Cruz to accept.

For these and other reasons, by 1996 the couple's relationship had soured for good, and Cruz moved back to New York. But by that time Jennifer had a new love. This was Ojani Noa, a Cuban-born waiter and aspiring model. The two had met while Jennifer was in Miami shooting *Blood and Wine*. At the time, Ojani was working at a trendy Cuban restaurant in Miami Beach, Larios, which was owned by Latina singing star Gloria Estefan.

Jennifer was immediately smitten, and they quickly became a couple. Ojani accompanied the actress back to Los Angeles when her work on *Blood and Wine* was complete. This new love interest was just one indication that dramatic new chapters in Jennifer's life, both personal and professional, were about to unfold. In just a few years, she had gone from being an unknown New York dancer, scuffling for her next job, to being a bright young Hollywood star-in-the-making. Great things were in store for Jennifer.

Selena and More

Back in L.A., Jennifer continued to work steadily, her reputation and paychecks increasing with each new opportunity. Her next film, released in 1997, was a surprising choice to some observers. It was a low-budget, deliberately cheesy-looking action-adventure film called Anaconda. Costarring with Jon Voight, Ice Cube, and Eric Stoltz, Jennifer plays the director of a documentary film crew on the Amazon River that gets entangled with a tribe of snake-worshipping natives and an insane snake hunter who is in search of a giant, deadly anaconda.

Jennifer had mixed feelings about her experience with *Anaconda*. She hated being on a location shoot in the Amazon region, so far from civilization and home. Yet Jennifer liked the finished film and thoroughly enjoyed taking part in a slam-bang action movie, especially in doing her own stunts. "It was a major bruise movie," she admits, "[but] I love action movies. I would be an action star—if I had the opportunity—in a minute."[37]

Anaconda got terrible reviews from critics, but it was a huge hit with audiences. In fact, it was briefly the number one box office movie in the country. When it reached the top spot, the film it knocked from first place was *Liar Liar,* a comedy that starred Jim Carrey, another alumnus of *In Living Color.*

MAKING A *U TURN*

Jennifer was next chosen over several other actresses, including Sharon Stone, for a starring role in the thriller *U Turn.* This movie, also released in 1997, had a great team behind it. It had an outstanding director, Oliver Stone, and it costarred Sean Penn and Nick Nolte, with a memorable supporting role from another gifted actor, Billy Bob Thornton. In the movie, a drifter and gambler (Penn) is stranded in a small desert town. He becomes dangerously involved with a powerful rich man (Nolte) and his abused wife (Jennifer) when each of them asks him to murder the other.

Jennifer almost did not make this movie. Several years earlier, she had had a disastrous audition with Stone for another movie. Jennifer recalls:

> The minute I began reading this long, four-page scene, he started walking around the room. Then he began rearranging the furniture. I'm like, 'What is he doing? This is so rude.' Well, he rearranged his entire office, and when I finished, the casting director said, 'Oliver?' and he turns and goes, 'Oh—um, OK. So you're a regular on that TV series?' And I go, 'Yeah.' And I left. I told my manager, 'I've never been treated like this and I never want to work for Oliver Stone.'[38]

So Jennifer refused to audition for *U Turn.* However, when the director personally called to apologize for his earlier rudeness, she changed her mind. She was glad she did. She felt that working with Nolte and Penn was a valuable education. "I could never work with better actors,"[39] she said. As for Stone, she comments, "Oliver . . . intimidated me at first. It was like, 'If you don't have an opinion on something, you'd better get one!' But he was totally respectful and always listened to me."[40] The director, for his part, praised Jennifer's resilience: "She's a tough chick. She was barefoot for days with fake blood on her."[41]

THE ROLE OF A LIFETIME COMES ALONG

In *U Turn*, Jennifer played a Native American woman. In *Blood and Wine*, her character was Cuban. In *Jack*, though her ethnicity was irrelevant to the story, she played Miss Marquez. All along, however, Jennifer had always focused on creating an acting career independent of her heritage.

Of course, she was proud of being Latina, but she was determined to not be known for playing *only* Latina characters. She told a reporter, "I never thought of myself as a Latina actress. You think about being an actress. The fact that my career is now moving in that direction makes me very proud."[42]

Yet Jennifer was not opposed to playing Latina roles, a philosophy that served her well because next up for Jennifer was the role of a lifetime. It was a very special Latina role about a famous, fanatically loved, real-life singer. This was a part playing pop superstar Selena Quintanilla Pérez, known to her millions of fans as Selena.

Selena, raised in Corpus Christi, Texas, performed a vibrant style of dance music called Tejano with her family band. She began her career when still a young girl and had made her first album at the age of 12. Selena soon became famous far beyond the Texas-Mexico border region where Tejano developed. But in 1995, when Selena was just 23 years old and on the verge of international stardom, tragedy struck. The ex-president of her fan club, who was about to be exposed for stealing from Selena's family, murdered her.

Jennifer appeared opposite Jack Nicholson *(shown)* in 1996's *Blood and Wine,* a crime-drama/dark comedy that costarred Michael Caine and was directed by Bob Rafelson. At this time, Jennifer was gaining the attention of Hollywood producers, and by 2000 she would have appeared in films with box-office heavyweights such as Owen Wilson, Sean Penn, Vince Vaughn, Robin Williams, and Bill Cosby.

FINDING THE RIGHT "MAGICAL PERSONALITY"

A few years later, Selena's father, Abraham Quintanilla Jr., was producing a biopic, or a biographical movie, about his much-loved daughter. Gregory Nava, who had directed Jennifer in *Mi Familia/My Family,* was set to direct it. Both men knew that choosing the right actress for the lead role would be crucial.

Whoever was picked would have to capture Selena's rebellious, proud spirit. Nava told the *Los Angeles Daily News* at the time, "Selena is just this deep phenomenon, people love her. You've got to look at why. Of course, there was her magical personality. But the key to Selena was that she accepted herself. We're always taught, as Latinos, that to make it in America you have to hide your true self. She did just the opposite, and was accepted bigger than anybody."[43]

Nava's search to find the right actress was extensive. He and Selena's father knew that her fans would protest strongly if the choice was bad. So they held auditions around the country, attracting 22,000 hopefuls. This huge group was quickly narrowed down to seven finalists.

Of these, three were nonactresses and four were professionals. Jennifer was one of the latter. She recalls, "Abraham . . . wanted to make sure he had the right person. It was a

LIFE AND ART INTERTWINE

Jennifer felt a strong kinship with Selena when she took on playing the life of the slain singer. Although she came from a much different background, Jennifer was able to connect to Selena's legacy and spirit in a powerful way. She comments, "Being Latino in this country, we're all looked at the same. They don't look at us and go, 'She's Salvadoran,' or, 'She's Puerto Rican.' I grew up in the Bronx, she grew up in a working-class neighborhood in Texas, but where she was at when she passed away. . . . I know that we were going through a lot of the same things."*

Elsewhere, Jennifer has commented on the tendency people have to try and pigeonhole other people, especially celebrities, very quickly. "People are so quick to form an opinion of you when you're in my position," she says. "They want to figure you out in five minutes, and there's no way you can do that. People take one look at me or judge me on one thing I do and decide what I'm like. I'm not saying it's a good or bad thing, but that's the way it is."**

Sometimes for performers, life and art intermingle closely with each other. Jennifer says that that happened, to a degree, decision that went back and forth. They actually had a girl from the open call [auditions] who they liked, and who looked like Selena. I do not naturally look like her, though we have similar bodies. So it was between the two of us, and for whatever reasons, they decided to go with me."[44]

CREATING A CHARACTER

Being picked to play Selena was a major coup for Jennifer. She commented frequently that good roles for actresses were hard to come by, and that this was one. She remarked that she felt honored to have gotten the chance to do it. Yet she also knew that it was going to be difficult to convincingly play a real-life

after she finished making *Selena*. Her subject, a famous singer who died tragically young, brought up a lot of feelings for Jennifer. The subject matter caused her to reflect on the brevity of life and on her own chances for lasting romance with her then-boyfriend, Ojani Noa.

"People ask me if doing the movie changed my life, and I don't know," she says. "Ojani proposed to me just when we were wrapping the film, and, when I think about it, Selena's death was a reminder of life and what it's all about and how you never know what's going to happen, and how you'd better really live for today. If I hadn't been working on this movie, I don't know if I would have said yes to Ojani."[***]

*   Quoted in Barney Hoskyns, "Selena—Interview with Actress Jennifer Lopez." *Interview*, April 1997.
**   Quoted in Anthony Noguera, "Latin Lessons: *Out Of Sight* Star Jennifer Lopez Tells FHM the Ways a Man Can Make it into Her Good Books." *FHM*, December 1998.
*** Hoskyns.

Jennifer's big movie break came with the lead role in *Selena*, the true
story of Selena Quintanilla Pérez, a Texas-born Tejano singer who rose from
cult status to international stardom. Jennifer won Outstanding Actress in
a Feature Film from the American Latino Media Arts Awards for her stirring
performance. Here she appears in a scene from the movie with actor
Jon Seda.

person who had been so beloved, especially someone who had
died so recently. Clearly, it had to be done with sensitivity.
Jennifer commented at the time, "Selena was someone who
had not just tremendous talent but also a beautiful heart, and I
think that's what fans loved most about her. I know her mem-
ory's still fresh in their minds, so the most important thing for
me is to get it right."[45]

Part of Jennifer's job, therefore, was to study Selena care-
fully. For example, she watched videos to learn the way the
singer laughed, danced, and moved on stage. In so doing, she
tried to capture Selena's essence. "Selena was a spirit," Jennifer

commented. "Nothing was going to stop her. And I admire that kind of drive."[46]

Jennifer also changed her physical appearance for the role. She wore wigs to play Selena as a teen and a young adult, and she wore bold lipstick as Selena as an adult. Yet the filmmakers did not want Jennifer to imitate Selena's appearance too much. At first, they considered giving Jennifer a false nose to make her nose more like Selena's. They also thought about giving Jennifer tinted contact lenses to wear to make Jennifer's hazel eyes resemble Selena's dark brown eyes. In the end, however, these ideas were rejected.

The filmmakers also decided not to have Jennifer do her own singing during the musical parts of the movie. At that point in her career, Jennifer was known as an actress, not a singer. Also, the filmmakers knew that Selena's fans already knew her voice intimately. So Jennifer lip-synched the songs.

"SUDDENLY I WAS BEING RECOGNIZED EVERYWHERE"

Selena, shot in Mexico and Texas, was released in 1997. Although not a smash hit, it did reasonably well at the box office. More important than the amount of money it made, however, was that the film proved to be a watershed event in several ways. It was one of the few high-profile Hollywood movies with a Latino theme ever made, and it showed Latino characters in a positive manner. The relative success of the movie and the positive portrayal of the Latino characters helped pave the way for future productions. *Selena* dominated 1997's American Latino Media Arts (ALMA) awards, winning top honors for best film, actress, actor, and director.

The film also made Jennifer Lopez a genuine star. *Selena* was the breakthrough role that Jennifer had wanted for so long. Jennifer was widely praised for her performance, and she earned several honors, including a Golden Globe nomination, a Lasting Image award, a Lone Star Film & TV award, and the MTV Movie Award for Best Breakthrough Performance.

A number of prominent critics singled her out for praise. Typical of these was Roger Ebert, who wrote in the *Chicago Sun-Times* that Jennifer's role was "a star-making performance."[47] Lisa Schwartzbaum of *Entertainment Weekly* added, "The best thing going for *Selena* is Selena herself, played with verve, heart, and a great deal of grace by the increasingly busy Jennifer Lopez."[48]

Jennifer also set a landmark financial record with *Selena*. Her fee, $1 million, made her the highest-paid Latina actress to date, and she used some of salary to buy a new Cadillac for her mother, which she delivered wrapped in a big bow! Finally, the movie was a watershed event because it made Jennifer a familiar figure to several generations of movie fans. "*Selena* was a big movie for me," she comments. "Kids loved the movie and they introduced it to their parents and grandparents. Suddenly I was being recognized everywhere."[49]

A FIRST MARRIAGE

Selena clearly changed Jennifer's professional career forever. Her personal life also took a dramatic turn during this period. At the wrap party for *Selena* in October 1996, Jennifer's boyfriend, Ojani, grabbed a microphone from the musicians on the stand. (A wrap party is a celebration traditionally held when a movie finishes shooting.)

To Jennifer's shock, Ojani used the mike to propose to her in front of everyone. When the surprised, but pleased, actress said yes, Ojani dropped to one knee and put a diamond ring on her finger. A few months later, in February 1997, the couple married in front of an audience of 200 friends and family in Miami. It was the first marriage for either of them. The ceremony came during a rare moment of rest for the actress. It was held just after the opening of *Blood and Wine* and just before the openings of *Selena* and *Anaconda*. After the ceremonies, the couple honeymooned in Key West, Florida. This was a well-deserved vacation for Jennifer who had just finished acting in four feature films, back to back, with barely a rest.

OUT OF SIGHT

Jennifer's time off did not last long. She remarked during this period that she wanted to seize every opportunity to work when she could: "I didn't expect it to happen like this, wrapping one film and flying out to do a new one the next day. But I'm fresh enough and ambitious enough to stay up all night for the sake of a job. I'm not gonna take it easy. I want to do so much more when I'm getting these great opportunities."[50]

After her return from her brief honeymoon, Jennifer went straight back to work. A major high point of this period was the role that many people consider Jennifer's best performance ever—the starring role in the comedy-thriller *Out of Sight,* based on the novel by gifted writer Elmore Leonard. Jennifer bested a number of other high-profile actresses, including Sandra Bullock, for the role. It was a great job, paying $2 million. As with *Blood and Wine,* the movie boasted an A-team of collaborators. The talented Steven Soderbergh was the director, and George Clooney, now starting his movie career after the successful TV show *ER,* was Jennifer's costar.

In *Out of Sight,* Jennifer plays Karen Sisco, a U.S. federal marshal on the trail of Jack Foley (Clooney), a smooth bank robber who has broken out of prison. A cat-and-mouse game develops as the marshal chases her quarry while the two fall in love. The screenplay was exciting and the direction inventive. Meanwhile, the stars got to show off their comic timing and romantic heat. As a result, *Out of Sight* was a hit with both audiences and critics when it was released in 1998. Typical of the critical reaction was Owen Gleiberman of *Entertainment Weekly,* who noted, "Lopez, for all her Latina-siren voluptuousness, has always projected a contained coolness, and this is the first movie in which it fully works for her. As Sisco is lured into a romance with Foley, you can see her resolve melt in spite of itself."[51]

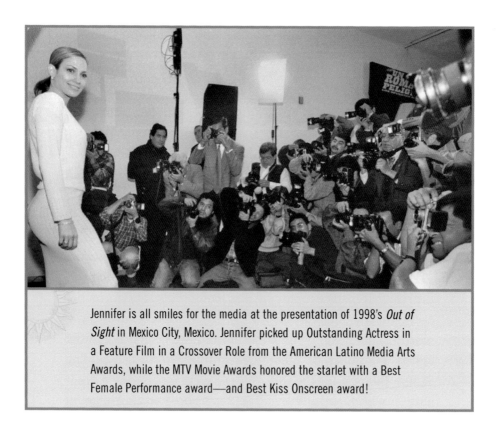

Jennifer is all smiles for the media at the presentation of 1998's *Out of Sight* in Mexico City, Mexico. Jennifer picked up Outstanding Actress in a Feature Film in a Crossover Role from the American Latino Media Arts Awards, while the MTV Movie Awards honored the starlet with a Best Female Performance award—and Best Kiss Onscreen award!

The character of Karen Sisco was another role in which Jennifer's ethnic heritage was irrelevant. Nonetheless, the press created a lot of hype around the fact that a Latina actress was starring in a major Hollywood movie. Director Steven Soderbergh downplayed this hype. He told a reporter, "It's not a question of, are people ready to see a Latina actress in big movies. The point is, people are ready to see Jennifer in high-profile movies. She's sexy, intelligent, beautiful but not implausibly beautiful, and she's got both really good instincts and very good technical chops [skills], which is rare."[52]

In 1998, Jennifer was also cast as one of the voices in the animated feature comedy *Antz*. She was in excellent company, starring with Woody Allen, Gene Hackman, Sharon Stone, Sylvester Stallone, and Anne Bancroft.

"PUT JENNIFER BACK ON THE PHONE"

That same year, Jennifer passed another milestone on her road to becoming a major star when she was invited to be a presenter at the Academy Awards ceremony. Several observers have commented that Jennifer was one of the few younger actresses that year who looked perfectly natural at the ceremony. She seemed to be always cool and calm, fitting in perfectly amid all the Oscar glamour.

At one point during the festivities, however, Jennifer lost her calm air. She remembers that after the ceremony, she walked into the green room, an area where presenters and other celebrities relaxed when not on stage. She recalls that it was packed with the likes of Alec Baldwin, Robert De Niro, Whoopi Goldberg, Sharon Stone, Warren Beatty, and Jack Nicholson. Jennifer was so overwhelmed when she first walked in that she had to walk back out. Then she was able to compose herself and walk back in.

In the green room, Jennifer called her mother at home in New York. She asked her mother if she had seen her on stage, and Mrs. Lopez replied yes, and that she had loved Jennifer's hair and dress. Then Jennifer handed the phone to Warren Beatty, whom she had just met, and asked him to say hello to her mother. When Mrs. Lopez asked who it was, the Hollywood icon told her his name. "Warren who?" Jennifer's mother asked. "Warren Beatty," he repeated. Assuming it was a joke, Mrs. Lopez said, "It is not! Put Jennifer back on the phone."[53]

A MARRIAGE GOES BAD

In many ways, 1998 was a tremendous year for Jennifer. She felt as though she was really hitting her stride as a performer, and her self-confidence, which was always strong, was becoming even greater. Asked by a reporter why she consistently got the juiciest Hollywood roles, she laughed and said, "Because I'm the best. I feel I can do anything—any kind of role. I'm fearless."[54]

BEING LATINA IN THE MOVIES

Jennifer was one of several singers and performers who came to fame during a surge of popular interest in Latin music in the 1990s and early 2000s. This surge of popularity will likely continue, since it has been estimated that by 2009 Latinos will surpass African Americans in numbers as the largest minority group in the United States.

Such popular acceptance of Latin entertainment has not always been the case. For example, a number of well-known actresses have had to downplay their Latin heritage in order to succeed. Among them were the Hollywood icons Rita Hayworth, who was born Margarita Carmen Dolores Cansino, and Raquel Welch, who was born Jo Raquel Tejada.

Today the situation is different, and Latin performers do not feel the need to undergo an "Anglo makeover" to be a success. Jennifer applauds this change because it gives the rest of the world an idea of Latin culture. She comments, "Now, the world is starting to see what it's like to grow up in a Latin family: the flavor and the culture and the passion and the music. We're a very passionate people."*

Jennifer has always been careful in her movie career to balance her roles, playing both specifically Latin characters and others where ethnicity is irrelevant. In Hollywood, she says, "People try to pigeonhole you. But I've always been very conscious of that when making choices. Even when I did television, I chose different types of roles, so they wouldn't be able to stereotype me. I realized that I had to fight that because I'm Latin."**

Elsewhere, she has commented, "I mean, what is a Latin spitfire? One of the things that [playing a non-Latin character] did was make people see me in a different light, in a role that wasn't constantly saying I was Latin. I was just a strong woman opposite a man, and that's always been a goal of mine. Which is not to say that if a Latin role came along I'd turn it down, because I'm more than proud of my heritage."***

Jennifer recalls a moment when she was talking with Oliver Stone, her director in *U-Turn*, about a new movie project he was working on. Jennifer says: "Oliver talked about the female role in the movie being perhaps for me, and said, 'Maybe the character could be Latin,' and I said, 'Whatever you do, don't make the character Latin because you're thinking of me to play it.' When the other producer said, 'Let's make her Greek, let's make her Italian,' I said, 'You know I have the chops [skills] to do that, Oliver.' And he took a few minutes to get there, even after I played an Apache Indian in his movie. I've said I want to be the Latina actress, but I also want to go beyond all that. I want to change things. Or at least, I can start that change."[†]

Despite Jennifer's Latino background, there was even some resistance to her being chosen for the lead role in *Selena*. Before shooting for the movie began, some people voiced the criticism that a Bronx-born Puerto Rican actress should not portray a Texas-born Chicana singer.

Jennifer was sensitive to these concerns, but she also felt that she had the acting ability to do the job right. She found it necessary to defend herself to the media and to the opposition of special-interest groups. "There was a lot of pressure," she recalls. "All the other roles I've gotten were like, you audition, you get the part, and that's it. This one was publicity-ridden from the first day. Suddenly my name was in the papers, and some people were happy and some weren't. I don't think it was personal toward me—at least I hope it wasn't. I tried to nip [the publicity] in the bud; you have to or it will get in the way of your work."[††]

From the very beginning, Jennifer felt a close and special kinship with the famous, charismatic singer she was playing. She felt that she had a lot in common with Selena, even though their lives had been very different. Jennifer comments, "Being Latino in this country, we're all looked at the same. They don't look at us and go, 'She's Salvadoran,' or, 'She's Puerto Rican.' I grew up in the Bronx, she grew up in a working-class neighborhood in Texas, but where she was at when she passed away. . . . I know that we were going through a lot of the same things."[†††]

* Quoted in Veronica Chambers and John Leland, "Lovin' La Vida Loca." *Newsweek*, May 31, 1999.

** Quoted in Sean Combs, "Touched by an Angel: Puff Daddy Interviews the Celestial Jennifer Lopez." *Notorious*, October 1999.

*** Quoted in Brantley Bardin, "1988 Woman of the Year: Jennifer Lopez." *Details*, December, 1998.

† Quoted in Joseph Hooper, "J.Lo Gets Right." *Elle*, September 2005.

†† Quoted in Barney Hoskyns, "Selena—Interview with Actress Jennifer Lopez." *Interview*, April 1997.

††† Ibid.

However, not every event in Jennifer's life that year was positive. When Jennifer had first brought Ojani to New York to meet her family, Lupe Lopez had commented, "I hope their marriage lasts as long as ours. Thirty-one years."[55] It was not to be. Rumors of friction between Jennifer and Ojani began to surface just months after their marriage, and they were divorced in March 1998, a little more than a year after the wedding.

Shortly after the divorce became final, Jennifer commented to a reporter that the blame, at least in part, was the same as with the dissolution of her relationship with David Cruz. Ojani was unable to deal with his wife's rising fame. She commented that, as with Cruz, she felt it was hard for a traditionally minded, macho man to accept that his wife earned more money than he did, that she wore sexy clothing, or that she played steamy love scenes with other actors.

Asked by a reporter what she had learned from the experience, Jennifer remarked, "That love isn't everything, it takes compromise and honesty and trust. Those are the most important things. If you don't have them, you don't have a relationship." Elsewhere she said, "I was young and naive and thought that love conquered the world—but you have to compromise to a certain extent. Sometimes people are just not ready to do that at that point in their lives."[56]

MORE SOUR NOTES

The breakup with Ojani was not the only sour note that year for Jennifer. As her fame grew, there were increasing numbers of reports of behavior problems. People complained that Jennifer was becoming hard to deal with, exhibiting the classic stereotypical behavior of a demanding, self-centered performer.

For example, a Universal Studios executive who worked on the marketing of *Out of Sight* said that making sure the actress showed up to promote the film at events such as TV talk shows was a full-time job. The executive commented,

"People would call up screaming at us, 'Where . . . is she?' Practically every show she did was like that. Everything had to get down to the wire."[57]

More unpleasant incidents followed. Jennifer showed up an hour late for a *Today Show* interview, and she also postponed a *Newsweek* interview three times before it was finally cancelled. More and more, the press began calling Jennifer a diva, although Jennifer has always insisted that she is not one. She comments, "I have a problem with the term. I feel like it means that you are mean to people, that you look down on people, and I'm not that type of person."[58]

A MISSTEP

Nevertheless, stories about her behavior persisted, and her habit of speaking her mind freely, perhaps another element of diva-like behavior, also got her into trouble. Jennifer's worst misstep was a 1998 interview that appeared in *Movieline* magazine.

In the interview, Jennifer spoke candidly, and not always kindly, about some of Hollywood's biggest actresses. Cameron Diaz was "a lucky model who's been given a lot of opportunities I just wish she would have done more with. She's beautiful and has a great presence, though, and in *My Best Friend's Wedding*, I thought, 'When directed, she can be good.'"[59] As for Gwyneth Paltrow, Jennifer commented, "Tell me what she's been in? I swear to God, I don't remember anything she was in. Some people get hot by association. I heard more about her and [then-boyfriend] Brad Pitt than I ever heard about her work."[60]

Jennifer bad-mouthed other actresses as well. On Winona Ryder, she said, "I was never a big fan of hers. In Hollywood she's revered, she gets nominated for Oscars, but I've never heard anyone in the public or among my friends say, 'Oh, I love her.' She's cute and talented, though, and I'd like her just for looking like my older sister, Leslie."[61] On Madonna, Jennifer claimed, "Do I think she's a great performer? Yeah. Do I think she's a great actress? No. Acting is what I do, so I'm harder on people when they say, 'Oh, I can do that—I can act.' I'm like, 'Hey, don't spit on my craft.'"[62]

MOVING ON

When the *Movieline* interview was published, the outcry over Jennifer's comments was immediate and strong. This backlash caught Jennifer by surprise, and it taught her a valuable lesson about speaking her mind in public. She later remarked, "[Now] I absolutely watch what I say more. I make my point, and I don't say much else."[63]

Some of Jennifer's colleagues and friends came to her defense. George Clooney, for instance, was sympathetic, noting that everyone makes mistakes early in a career: "There should really be someone who gives you lessons about fame and teaches you what to say and what not to do. You can't just say what's on your mind, and whatever's true today might not be true 15 minutes from now," he said. [64] Jennifer later apologized, both publicly and privately, for her candid statements. She also tried to ignore the criticism because she had other things to think about. She wanted to move on to something new. Specifically, she wanted to concentrate on a new goal of creating a singing career.

Jennifer's portrayal of Selena had reawakened an interest in singing, something she had ignored for years. In particular, she says, the opening scene of *Selena*, when she performs in front of a huge audience of ecstatic fans, was a revelation. Jennifer was just acting the role of a famous singer, of course, but nonetheless the excitement of the crowd moved her. She jokes, "The first show I did, thirty-five thousand people showed up, and I liked it!"[65]

NO FEAR

Jennifer was an accomplished actor, but few actors have also had successful careers in music. Those who have succeeded, such as Barbra Streisand, Diana Ross, Will Smith, and Whitney Houston, have generally established themselves as singers before branching into acting. Those who have tried to go the other direction have not been as successful. Don Johnson, Cybill Shepherd, and Bruce Willis are just three successful actors whose attempts at musical careers flopped badly. Many of Jennifer's friends and fans, as well as others in the industry, were skeptical of her move to singing.

Jennifer had modeled herself on Streisand for years, considering the star an example of someone who could be wildly successful in multiple areas of entertainment. Jennifer has frequently spoken of her admiration for the singer/actress/director, claiming that other than her mother and father, who gave her the values of hard work, Barbra Streisand was a role model for her. Jennifer looks up to Streisand as an actor, singer, and director who does not compromise her choices, and being a singer and an actress herself, Jennifer realizes that both talents can be performed and maintained at a high level.

Jennifer was aware of the risks in starting a new, parallel career, yet she was not afraid. As she contemplated this new chapter in her life, a reporter asked her if the prospect of failing as a singer frightened her. She laughed and replied, "How can I live my life in fear like that? The winners take risks. That's the only way to be."[66]

Becoming
a Diva

Her role in *Selena* had inspired Jennifer to try singing. It also made her feel her Latin roots especially strongly. Motivated by her experience, Jennifer cut a Spanish-language demo, or "demonstration" record, designed to feature a song or singer's voice. She then began negotiating with record companies about making an album.

The move was well timed. In the 1990s, a number of singers and musicians with Latin roots, including Ricky Martin, Christina Aguilera, Gloria Estefan, Carlos Santana, Enrique Iglesias, and Marc Anthony, were enjoying a huge surge in popularity in the United States. Latin-based pop was topping the sales charts, and many people in the industry were predicting a bright future for the genre. Asked by a reporter if this was a good time to be Latin, Jennifer mischievously replied, "It's always a good time to be Latin."[67]

PREPARING THE DEBUT ALBUM

Sony Records, one of the giants in the recording industry, signed Jennifer to a recording contract and promised to give her album a big promotional push. She had very specific ideas about what she wanted. She recalls, "After signing with Sony, I discussed how I wanted the record to sound. I was played many songs, by artists ranging from [singer/songwriter/producer] Babyface to [songwriter] Diane Warren, but I felt it was important that my record be less pop and have more urban Latin appeal. Of course, that took a little explaining."[68]

Jennifer called her style of music "Latin soul," a mixture of all the influences she had absorbed over the years. She described it as "a kind of hybrid—the music somebody like me would like, who grew up in the Bronx, of Latin descent but a very American family."[69] Most of the songs were in English and were written mainly by established, powerhouse songwriters such as Emilio Estefan, although Jennifer also tried her hand at writing. "You have to have heightened emotions," she says of the songwriting process. "If you're really happy, angry, depressed or in love, you can write a good song."[70]

For Jennifer, singing has always had certain similarities to acting. In both, she says, she tries to convey emotions and tell stories to her audiences. While working on the album, Jennifer commented on this and confessed to a little concern over how it would be received: "I've been trying to discover what works, to tap into the emotion and drama that I bring into my acting. And believe me, there has always been a lot of praying on my part."[71]

A SMASH

Jennifer's debut album, *On the 6,* received generally poor critical response when it was released in 1999. David Browne, a reviewer for *Entertainment Weekly*, stated, "How sad that so much of this year's Latin-music boom had so little to do with Latin music. . . . This appallingly pallid set of vanilla ballads, limp rap, and diluted fiesta pop [*On the 6*] was an insult not just to Latin music but to music in general."[72] Other critics chimed in with their opinions, adding that the songwriting was "mediocre" and Jennifer's voice "thin and ordinary."

Yet the performer's fans did not agree with the critics. *On the 6* was an immediate smash success. The album's first single, "If You Had My Love," became a number one hit, and its sexy video was also a major hit on MTV. The album peaked at number eight, was in the top twenty for 11 weeks, and stayed on the best-seller charts for 53 weeks. *On the 6* also produced

THE STARDOM GLOW

In the years since she became a genuine star, many observers have remarked on Jennifer's ability to project the kind of glamour that Hollywood actresses of previous decades had. She says that it comes from emulating those stars:

I have the 'stardom glow.' See, I grew up watching real movie stars—Ava Gardner, Rita Hayworth, Marilyn Monroe. Glamorous women like those are why I wanted to get into the business. And from the time I first started off as an actress, each day I had an audition, I'd wake up, do my hair and my makeup, look at myself in the mirror and say, 'I have the stardom glow today.' A lot of people go into meetings and auditions all nervous. No! You've got to have WOW! I tell my actress friends this all the time. I walk into auditions going, 'What's gonna make me different from all the other girls here?' [The answer is that] they're looking for the next star to walk into that room. It's about being alive, open, electric, confident. That's the 'wow.'*

Becoming an instantly recognized star, Jennifer quickly found, is a two-edged sword. There were times when she loved the attention, and there were times when she hated it. "Every several more hit singles, and the album eventually sold more than three million copies in the United States and seven million worldwide.

Jennifer's debut album also earned a number of awards, notably a 2000 Grammy nomination for Best Dance Performance for "Waiting for Tonight," the second single from the album. Meanwhile, a Spanish-language duet with Marc Anthony from the album, "No Me Ames," received two nominations at the Latin Grammy Awards ceremony that year. Another single, "Let's Get Loud," earned Jennifer a second Grammy nomination in 2001.

day, if you go shopping at Barneys or something, you know the paparazzi will be out there. So you better have your nice jeans on, your boots, your nice little ensemble, your glasses—it's all a lot of work. I'm not complaining though; it's a lot of fun too."[**] Elsewhere, she has commented:

It gave me a lot of anxiety when I began to get so much more recognized. It was like, 'What . . . have I done? Have I made a deal with the devil here?' This stuff of people invading your life, like when you're eating at a restaurant or just walking around, it freaks you out. You're like, I don't want that person coming up to me to ask for an autograph. But if you're stressed, you attract it even more. It's just easier not to fight things so much. . . . It's easier to just sign the autograph quick instead of turning it into a bigger thing. Now I step back and go, 'Hey, I'm from the Bronx, I'm tough and I'm not going to let this get to me.'[***]

[*]   Quoted in Stephen Rebello, "The Wow." *Movieline*, February 1998.
[**] Quoted in Martha Frankel, "Jennifer Lopez Loves To . . ." *Cosmopolitan*, March 1999.
[***] Rebello.

Jennifer and Sean "Puffy" Combs arrive for the first annual Latin Grammy Awards in Los Angeles in September 2000. Jennifer's good-girl image was temporarily tarnished in December 1999 when she and Combs were arrested following a shooting at a New York City nightclub. In 2001, the two announced their breakup.

"THE DRESS"

The 2000 Grammy ceremonies were not only significant for Jennifer's nomination. The awards that year also celebrated, more generally, the rising wave of Latin-tinged pop in the United States. Carlos Santana, the veteran Mexican-born rock guitarist, dominated that year's awards with his album *Supernatural*. Christina Aguilera, whose father is from Ecuador, was named Best New Artist, and a number of other Latin artists were recognized in other categories as well.

The televised ceremonies that year were notable for something else as well: Jennifer's outfit. She presented an award wearing a green Versace dress that was daringly sheer and very revealing. "The Dress," as it became known, was instantly famous. A photo of Jennifer wearing it was downloaded more than 600,000 times from the official Grammy Web site in the first 24 hours after it was put up.

"The Dress" became the subject of countless stories in the media, jokes by comedians, and other forms of attention. To reporters who have asked her about the notorious garb, Jennifer has always teasingly insisted that it was no big deal and that she did not realize what a fuss it would cause. She says, "I wore it because it was just a nice dress."[73]

THE SHOOTING

The furor over "The Dress" was just one aspect of Jennifer's growing fame. As she became better known, her life was increasingly becoming fodder for nonstop gossip and breathless media coverage. At the turn of the twenty-first century, it seemed as though every magazine, newspaper, and television news show in the world featured Jennifer.

The media especially loved to report and speculate on Jennifer's new love affair. In the wake of her breakup with Ojani, she had begun a relationship with rapper and entertainment mogul Sean Combs, better known by one of his many nicknames: Puff Daddy, P. Diddy, or (as Jennifer usually called him) Puffy.

The couple insisted they were just friends for a long time, before finally admitting that they were romantically involved. Although they dated for two and a half years and were constantly in the media spotlight, one evening in particular stands out in the public mind. It happened late in 1999, when Jennifer and Puffy were involved in a shooting at Club New York in midtown Manhattan.

One of the people in Combs's party, a protégée of the rapper named Shyne, fired a gun inside the club, and in the ensuing chaos, three people were injured. Jennifer and Puffy were trying to leave as police reached the scene. According to witnesses, their car went through 10 red lights before being stopped. While investigating, the police found a stolen, loaded handgun in Combs's car.

THE BREAKUP

The police arrested Combs as well as the car's driver, Wardel Fenderson, and a bodyguard, Anthony "Wolf" Jones. At first, Jennifer was charged with illegal gun possession. The charges were eventually dropped against her but not before she was handcuffed and detained in a police station for 14 hours. Accounts differ wildly about her behavior during this period. According to some sources, she cried the whole time. Other accounts say she acted imperiously, demanding that policemen run errands for her such as fetching some hand cream. Still other reports claim that she was simply in quiet control of herself.

The charges against Puffy were not dropped, and he later endured a two-month trial. He was accused of illegal gun possession as well as bribery because the rapper's driver, Fenderson, claimed that Combs offered him cash and a diamond ring to say that the gun was his. According to CourtTV documents, Fenderson testified, "Mr. Combs . . . turned to me and he whispered in a hushed voice. His exact words were, 'I will give you $50,000 to say the gun was yours.' He said, 'I'm Puff Daddy, I can't take this gun.'"[74]

Combs was eventually acquitted of the charges. The incident, however, took its toll on his relationship with Jennifer. The especially intense media attention was probably at least partly to blame. News reports were not kind to Combs during this time, playing up his reputation for violence and danger. Those same news reports and commentary were generally sympathetic to Jennifer. Writer Kathleen Tracy notes, "The media generally stuck to the theme of 'What's a nice girl like this doing with a bad guy like that?'"[75]

Jennifer may have felt that associating with Combs was permanently hurting her reputation. As a close friend of Jennifer's told *Newsweek*, "The people around her have repeatedly told her that you can't be Hollywood's sweetheart if you're running from the cops."[76] In any case, Jennifer's relationship with the rapper was over by Valentines Day, 2001.

MIXED SUCCESS IN THE MOVIES

Jennifer had taken a long break from the movies while working on her album. When she returned to her film career, the results were mixed. First she costarred with Vince Vaughn in a scary science-fiction thriller, *The Cell*, in 2000. In this movie, Jennifer plays a psychologist who is trying to learn the secrets of a serial killer. In a desperate race to save his latest victim, the psychologist uses an experimental procedure to literally enter the killer's mind.

The movie was visually adventurous, but it got mediocre reviews and attracted only small audiences. Many of Jennifer's fans were turned off by the movie's violence and strong sexual imagery. Jennifer defended her choice of accepting the role, however, pointing out to a reporter that *The Cell* was intended for adults: "This film certainly is not meant for the girls who sing along with my songs."[77]

Jennifer did much better, at least financially, with a romantic comedy that came out early in 2001. *The Wedding Planner*, costarring Matthew McConaughey, shot to the number one spot at the box office during its first week of release.

"SISTER FACE"

Several powerful movers and shakers in the world of music have helped Jennifer with songwriting, production, and other aspects of her musical career. One of them is Emilio Estefan. Estefan, who along with his wife, Gloria, has been the driving force behind the Miami Sound Machine.

Estefan has worked with almost every major crossover Latino act at one time or another, so he has had a lot of experience. He says that in the beginning of his career, being Latino was nothing special. It took a younger generation that included Jennifer to turn Latin music into a popular form that received lots of attention and popular acclaim. He recalls that when he started, it was tough to be a Latino artist. Carlos Santana, Jose Feliciano, and other artists faced the same problem. Later, when singers like Jon Secada, Ricky Martin, Shakira, and Jennifer came in, it became easier because music industry people realized that there was a huge potential audience. Jennifer was thus an important part of the Latin music boom that made this acceptance possible.

Another person who helped Jennifer greatly early in her singing career was her vocal coach, the legendary soul singer Betty Wright. Wright has very warm feelings about her younger student. She says, "Since the first day we began working together I've called her Sister Face. It has two meanings: First, she is so cute, but at the same time Jennifer doesn't have a problem facing down any issues that might bother her. There are folks who will backstab or talk when you're not around, but Jennifer will face anything. She also has to be one of the most spiritual persons I've ever met."*

Although she has the ability to face the big issues, it is always reassuring, even to a confident personality like Jennifer, to have a supportive network of friends around. In 1998, Jennifer gave an interview to *Movieline* magazine in which she spoke frankly about what she saw as faults in several other actresses. Jennifer was widely attacked in the media for this forthright but hurtful interview. She admitted later that it was not a very politically correct move. She commented, "Maybe I was a little bit careless. . . I'm not a perfect person. I make mistakes. . . . [But] I follow my heart. That's the one thing I can say about myself."**

Meanwhile, in the aftermath of the incident, a number of the actress's colleagues and friends came to her defense. One of the most vocal was George Clooney, who had recently costarred with her in the thriller *Out of Sight*. Clooney was publicly sympathetic toward his costar. "Jennifer is great," he told a reporter. "She was just starting to get things going and then she had that *Movieline* article, which kind of jinxed her. . . . But you learn as you go. She had to battle after the *Movieline* incident and it was really fun to be around her then because she's a real fighter. She's a nice girl and she's also talented and smart. She stepped into a place that put her where she had to struggle hard and she coped really well."***

Another supportive figure in Jennifer's life was her first serious boyfriend, David Cruz. The couple met when she was still in high school, and he moved to Los Angeles soon after she relocated there for her job as a Fly Girl on the *In Living Color* television show.

Their relationship eventually fizzled. According to Jennifer, this was in part because he never really found a promising career while he was on the West Coast with her. While their connection was still strong, however, he always remained loyal to Jennifer and her goals. He defended her when other people questioned her goals and dreams. She recalls of Cruz,

We started dating when I was 15 and dated only each other for nine years. . . . We lived in the same neighborhood and he'd see me in, like, a weird hat, wearing something I'd cut together from a picture I'd seen in a magazine and I'd be just going to the track to run. I was creating my own style. Everybody would look at me, like I was a nerd, 'What is she doing? What is she wearing?' Because people didn't do that in my neighborhood. People didn't work out or take care of their bodies. If people see you striving for things, it threatens them. I was into, 'This two-bit town isn't big enough for me.' My boyfriend would say, 'Jennifer has bigger plans.'†

*   Quoted in Michael A. Gonzales, "Jennifer's Many Phases." *Latina*, March 1999.

**   Quoted in Stephen Rebello, "The Wow." *Movieline*, February 1998.

*** Quoted in Martyn Palmer, "Jennifer Lopez." *Total Film*, December 1998.

†   Quoted in Joseph Hooper, "J.Lo Gets Right." *Elle*, September 2005.

In this light comedy, Jennifer plays a wedding planner who has no romantic life of her own. Then she falls in love with a man who saves her life only to find that he is the intended groom in a big wedding she is planning.

DRAMAS

That same year, 2001, Jennifer again changed directions and starred in an unusual romantic drama, *Angel Eyes*. In it, she plays a tough Chicago cop who is saved from an ambush by a loner, played by the intense actor Jim Caviezel, who believes he is her guardian angel. The two gradually fall in love and begin to drop the emotional barriers they have built around themselves. *Angel Eyes* was another disappointment, garnering only lukewarm reviews and box office profits.

Yet this did not stop Jennifer from continuing to try her hand at serious dramas. In 2002, she starred in *Enough*, as a waitress who is being cheated on and abused by her new husband. Fearing for the safety of herself and her daughter, Jennifer's character tries to run away. When her husband finds her, she is forced to violently fight back. The movie bombed at the box office, despite a talented supporting cast and director and the sight of Jennifer learning and using Krav Maga, a self-defense technique used by the Israeli military. Critics were not kind to it either. Typical was the reviewer for the *Dallas Morning News*, who wrote, "Spousal abuse is a major problem in contemporary society, but the film reduces this domestic tragedy to florid [elaborate] melodrama."[78]

J TO THA L-O!

While she was making these films, Jennifer did not abandon her musical career. In 2001, she released *J.Lo*, a second album of "Latin soul," titled after the nickname she was then using. Some reviewers liked it a lot. The critic for *SonicNet*, for example, wrote, "*J.Lo* has a feisty, damn-I-know-I'm-all-that attitude, combined with pulsating, insistent beats that leap out of the speakers and make you wanna move."[79]

Other critics did not like it. They felt that Jennifer was just providing more of the same as before, with little originality or spice. A reviewer in *All Music Guide* remarked, "Essentially, this is the same album as *On the Six*, only a little longer with a little less focus and not as many memorable songs. This lack of winning singles becomes a drag, since at over an hour, the record meanders much longer than it should."[80]

Once again, however, Jennifer's fans were completely at odds with the critics. *J.Lo* was an even bigger hit than her debut album. The album entered the pop sales charts at number one and in time sold four million copies in the United States and 12 million worldwide. Among the hit singles from the album were "Love Don't Cost a Thing," "Play," and "Ain't It Funny."

The nearly simultaneous release of *The Wedding Planner* and *J.Lo* made history. Thanks to the instant success of both, Jennifer became the first actress/singer ever to have both a movie and a music album in the number-one spots in the same week. Jeff Blake, an executive at Columbia TriStar, the studio that made the movie, commented, "It is a rare star who can claim the No. 1 movie and the No. 1 album in the same week, but Jennifer is one of those talents who can do it all."[81]

J.Lo was such a huge success that Jennifer was inspired to remix the album and release the result. This album, *J to tha L-O!: The Remixes*, was released in 2002 and featured collaborations with, among other artists, Puffy Combs, Ja Rule, and 50 Cent. Like its predecessor, *J to tha L-O!: The Remixes* was another huge hit. It debuted at the number-one spot, the first remix album to do so, and became not only one of the best-selling remix albums in the United States but the third best-selling remix album of all time worldwide.

NEW VENUES

Jennifer was on a real roll now, and during this period she branched out in several directions beyond film and music. For example, she starred in a television concert special called "Let's

Get Loud," taped on two sold-out nights at Roberto Clemente Stadium in Carolina, Puerto Rico. Some fans and critics criticized Jennifer for lip-synching portions of the concert, but it was still a success. It was the number-one show in its time slot, with a full-length version of the concert later released on DVD.

Jennifer was also on television to host an episode of *Saturday Night Live* early in 2001. In one of the show's sketches, she made fun of her reputation as a difficult diva. In another, she appeared as a World War II-era singer, entertaining military troops in a free performance. Following the terrorist attacks of September 11, 2001, later that year, Jennifer played a similar role in real life when she entertained U.S. troops in freezing weather at an American Air Force base in Germany, on a bill with Kid Rock and Ja Rule.

The singer/actress was also branching out with new business ventures during this period. One was a series of lucrative endorsements for products such as Coke and L'Oreal cosmetics. Another was Madre's, an upscale Latin-themed restaurant that she opened in Pasadena, California. Jennifer's grandmother's cooking, as well as Cuban and other Latin foods, inspired the dishes that were served at the eatery. The historic old sections of Havana, Cuba, inspired the restaurant's lavish interior decoration.

MORE ROMANCE GONE BAD

After Jennifer's breakup with Puffy Combs, she was romantically linked with a number of men. In fact, since she was a teenager Jennifer had never liked being without romance. She once commented, "I've always had a huge fear of dying or becoming ill. The thing I'm most afraid of, though, is being alone, which I think a lot of performers fear. It's why we seek the limelight—so we're not alone, we're adored. We're loved, so people want to be around us. The fear of being alone drives my life."[82]

Soon there would be another new man in her life. This was Texas-born dancer Cris Judd, whom she met when he worked

Jennifer and second husband, Cris Judd, arrive for the grand opening of her family's new Latin restaurant, Madre's, in Pasadena, California, in April 2002. The Lopez family-run business, which serves hearty Latin-tinged dishes, opened with a star-studded party that was attended by Kobe Bryant, Nicole Kidman, Jay Leno, and Christian Slater.

on her video "Love Don't Cost a Thing." They were married in Calabasas, California, in September 2001, in a ceremony in front of 170 friends and family. It was Cris's first marriage.

Together they started building a spacious mansion in the Hollywood Hills. Very soon after the ceremony, however, rumors of trouble began flying in the media as they had with Jennifer's first marriage. The most persistent of these rumors indicated a budding relationship between Jennifer and actor Ben Affleck.

Affleck, three years younger than Jennifer, by coincidence shares a birthday with Cris Judd. Ben grew up in Cambridge, Massachusetts, near Boston, and first became famous as part of a writing and acting partnership with Matt Damon. He met Jennifer while they were costarring in a gangster comedy called *Gigli*. For that role, Jennifer had replaced Halle Berry who had originally been slated to appear.

The rumors that Affleck was romantically interested in Jennifer were fueled by an incident that happened at a press event at Madre's. Seemingly from nowhere, a mysterious man appeared and gave Jennifer a beautiful bouquet of flowers from Affleck, even as her husband, Cris Judd, stood by.

HIGH AND LOW POINTS

When word began to leak out about a possible romance between Jennifer and Ben, the media jumped all over the story. The burning question was on everyone's mind: Was Jennifer having an affair while she was married? Both Jennifer and Ben denied it fiercely, but the rumors persisted. Meanwhile, her marriage deteriorated, and Jennifer and Cris separated in the summer of 2002. On July 25, 2002, the day after her thirty-second birthday, Jennifer was caught passionately kissing Affleck. On that day, she filed for divorce from Cris Judd. The divorce settlement allegedly cost Jennifer $15 million. Jennifer's breakup was not the only bad news she had during this period. Arlene Rodriguez, Jennifer's personal assistant for years, resigned. Arlene had been Jennifer's friend since childhood, when they had known each other at Holy Family Elementary School.

There were bright spots, however, in Jennifer's life during this period too. One was Jennifer's 2002 purchase of an eight-bedroom waterfront mansion on Fisher Island in Biscayne

Bay, off Miami, Florida. The 10,800-square-feet-estate cost a reported $9.5 million. It was about eight blocks down the street from the home of another Latin singing star, Ricky Martin.

Jennifer had fallen in love with Miami when she was shooting *Blood and Wine* and had promised herself she would have a home there someday. "After I was there three days," she recalls, "I knew I was going to live there. I just felt like home. I love the culture of that town— it's very Latino. I love the sunshine and the humidity. I love being that close to the water, and I love that beachy feeling. For me, the hotter the better."[83]

ANOTHER ONE-TWO PUNCH

Jennifer scored another one-two punch in her professional career in 2002. Late in the year, she released her third album of new material, *This Is Me . . . Then*. While its sales were not as red-hot as those of her earlier albums, it nonetheless reached number two on the pop charts and spawned four hit singles. Her musical career was boosted further that year when she won multiple awards, including a World Music Award for World's Best-Selling Latin Female Artist, an MTV Video Music Award for Best Hip-Hop Video (for "I'm Real"), a VH1/Vogue Fashion Award for Most Influential Artist, and an MTV Europe Music Award for Best Female.

At the same time, Jennifer's latest film, *Maid in Manhattan*, for which she was paid $12 million, proved to be a huge box office hit. In fact, it has been Jennifer's most popular film in the United States to date. *Maid in Manhattan* was another romantic comedy, costarring the distinguished British actor Ralph Fiennes. In the movie, Fiennes plays an American political hopeful who falls in love with Jennifer's character, a single mother who works as a maid at a top New York hotel.

BENNIFER

Meanwhile, the Lopez-Affleck relationship was irresistible to the media, which delighted in covering the couple it called

"Bennifer." Now that it was in the open, the romance dominated entertainment gossip throughout the year.

The couple officially announced their engagement in November 2002. To celebrate, Ben gave Jennifer a six-carat pink diamond ring worth a reported $1.2 million. The couple shared the news of their engagement on national television, appearing with Diane Sawyer on ABC's *Primetime: Special Edition.*

On that show, Jennifer remarked how seemingly unalike, yet alike, the two were, commenting, "We've talked about this so many times, and we talked about how people kind of see him with . . . one type of person and me with another type of person, and the two of us together is like, 'How did that happen?' And how we're probably more alike and from the same kind of background . . . same kind of upbringing and same kind of family and same kind of house."[84]

GIGLI

Bennifer's romance was in full swing, but *Gigli,* the movie that had introduced the couple to each other, had yet to come out. The studio had delayed the film's release date, apparently because test audiences had hated its lumbering, leaden attempts at comedy. The film was reshot and re-edited, but this repair work proved unsuccessful.

When it was finally released in 2003, *Gigli* became one of Hollywood's most notorious turkeys. It cost $54 million to make and only returned a fraction of that in ticket and DVD sales. Critics howled at it, audiences stayed away, and *Gigli* has since appeared prominently on a number of "worst movie" lists. Jennifer's performance also won the dubious honor of Worst Actress in the annual satirical Golden Raspberry Razzie Awards.

Nonetheless, Jennifer loyally defended the film. She commented, "I've seen a lot worse movies. It was like the media had a field day. Sometimes I think the media is like high school, like a clique: Sometimes they love this one popular girl,

Jennifer and then-fiancé Ben Affleck arrive hand-in-hand for the Academy Awards on March 23, 2003, in Los Angeles. The couple, nicknamed "Bennifer" by the press, became the target of a media frenzy that elevated the romance to worldwide attention. The marriage was called off hours before the couple was to be wed in September 2003, and in January 2004, publicists for the couple officially announced a permanent split for the twosome.

and then they hate her and make her the nerd. And then they love her again."[85]

The Bennifer romance continued despite the *Gigli* disaster. Lopez told one interviewer after another that Affleck was "the one" and that the couple would soon have a family. Furthermore, she said, after the marriage she planned to go by the name Jennifer Affleck both privately and professionally.

The wedding was planned for September 2003 in Santa Barbara. Just days before it was due to take place, however, Affleck was spotted partying with exotic dancers at a club in Vancouver, British Columbia, where he was filming *Paycheck* with Uma Thurman. Jennifer got the news when her own sister, a radio presenter, asked her live and on air about the news. Taken aback, Jennifer stuttered and replied, "It sounds like Ben. I'll have to ask him."[86]

THE END OF THE AFFAIR

Apparently, the stories of Affleck's partying were true. The wedding was called off just hours before it was to start, and it was unclear if it would be rescheduled at all. The world was left waiting for an answer until publicists for the two stars announced a permanent split in January of 2004. Once it was clear that the two were not going to be reconciled, a question arose. Would Jennifer give back the famous ring? (She did, eventually.) There were other dilemmas as well. Lasse Hallström, the Swedish-born director who was by then filming Jennifer in her next movie, *An Unfinished Life*, dryly remarked, "I still don't know what to do with the glass vase I bought as a wedding present. Maybe I'll give it to her at the opening of the film."[87]

As she had in the past, Jennifer weathered this rocky point in her personal life. In the years since, she has continued to work steadily and to develop as an individual. Recent years have seen her still a star, still creating, and still very much in the public eye.

6

An Unfinished Life

In terms of her professional work, the period following Jennifer's breakup with Ben Affleck was one of mixed highs and lows. For one thing, a second movie that she and Affleck had shot together, a sentimental romantic comedy called *Jersey Girl*, proved to be nearly as troublesome as Gigli had been.

Jersey Girl was shelved for a long time, probably in part because of the intense publicity over the couple's recent split. It was then heavily edited, reducing Jennifer's appearance to a cameo. In this new version, Jennifer's character dies in the first 15 minutes of the film, leaving her husband (Affleck, playing a workaholic music executive) to raise their young daughter alone. Liv Tyler plays Ben's new romantic interest in the movie. Released in 2004, *Jersey Girl* was generally panned by critics and avoided by audiences. It did not bomb as badly as *Gigli* had, but overall it was a disappointment.

REBIRTH

Jennifer's singing career was also stagnating somewhat during this period. By now, she had a high-powered new manager, Jeff Kwatinetz. Under his guidance, Jennifer switched labels, and in 2005 released a fourth studio album, *Rebirth*.

The album had a strong start on the sales charts, debuting at number two, while its major single, "Get Right," reached the top fifteen. Overall, however, *Rebirth* did not do as well as hoped. It sold 1.3 million copies in the United States and three million worldwide. These were very respectable figures but nowhere near the stratospheric sales of Jennifer's previous albums.

Although the album was a disappointment commercially, its musical message was close to Jennifer's heart. The album's songs emphasized a theme that she felt very passionate about at the moment: self-transformation, or the ability to change oneself. The title, *Rebirth*, thus had a special meaning for Jennifer because it signified her own rebirth, her own starting over.

Jennifer's desire to make a new start in her life and her art was partly due to the publicity-heavy life she had been living. She made it clear in interviews during this period that she wanted to create a new life for herself, one with fewer gossipy news headlines and more meaningful home life. She commented, "I'm an infant, but I feel like I'm in a good place. The past couple of years were very transitional, super-transitional for me. A lot of things happened professionally that shook me up. [At a point like that] you say, 'Something weird is happening,' and you step back and take a minute and you start over."[88]

NEW LOVE

Jennifer told a number of reporters that being single again helped her to reassess her life. In particular, she said, she realized the virtues of slowing down: "It [being single] forced me to take moments and do nothing," she commented. "It was

Jennifer and her husband, Marc Anthony, perform onstage together at the Grammy Awards in February 2005 in Los Angeles. Jennifer and Marc had once worked together in music videos and briefly dated in the late 1990s. The couple reunited and married in June 2004. Since then, they have recorded together and made the film *El Cantante*.

scary but great. What was good was that I realized I could be still and be okay. You get so used to moving, you wind up asking yourself, 'Have I [even] gone to the bathroom today? I haven't stopped to do anything.' It's crazy."[89]

Despite the relative peace she discovered in being single, that status did not last long. After only a few months of being unattached, Jennifer started dating a gifted singer named Marc Anthony. Anthony, like Jennifer, was born in New York City of Puerto Rican immigrant parents. He was the same singer with whom she had recorded *"No Me Ames,"* the much-praised Spanish-language song on her first album.

(Marc may have been predestined to sing. His parents, Felipe and Guillermina Muñiz, named him Marco Antonio Muñiz after a popular Mexican-born singer of that name. Marc later adopted the stage name Marc Anthony to avoid confusion.)

At the time he began dating Jennifer, Anthony was married to a former Miss Universe, Puerto Rican-born actress Dayanara Torres. They had two young children, Cristian and Ryan, and Anthony had a daughter, Arianna, from an earlier relationship. After he began seeing Jennifer, he filed for divorce, and on June 5, 2004, four days after the divorce became final, he and Jennifer married. The ceremony was a secret. There were only 35 guests, and all of them thought they were simply attending an afternoon party at Jennifer's Beverly Hills house.

Despite the secrecy, the ceremony quickly became public knowledge, making the news in a bizarre way in fall 2004. Anthony's car was stolen, and in it was his laptop computer, which contained a video of the wedding. Two men were later charged with trying to ransom it back to the couple for $1 million.

OUT OF THE SPOTLIGHT

Some of Jennifer's previous loves had relished the public's attention she attracted. Marc Anthony, however, treasures his privacy and, when he is off the stage, he tries to avoid the spotlight. In fact, for a long time he did not even publicly admit that he had remarried. The new marriage seems to have worked in a similar way for Jennifer, making her less eager to be in the public eye. "I was a workaholic," she says, "and I have to admit that getting married made me calm down a bit."[90] She also comments:

> The lifestyle just gets to you after a while. I mean, it can be great, it can be exciting, but it's just totally full on. It takes over everything else, and soon it all becomes too much. I decided to get off the spinning carousel ride. It was a definite choice I made and I have to say it was quite a scary one because, even though you know that you feel you want the madness to stop, once you stop it and get off, your first instinct is to panic and then jump right back on.[91]

Even though marriage to Anthony has calmed her down a bit, Jennifer's energy level remains high. She rarely stops moving, she says, but when she does, she does so completely. "I'm like an engine that is constantly on. But when I get a free day, then I do absolutely nothing. I stay in at home in my tracksuit, I sleep, spend hours on the phone talking to my mother and my friends."[92]

Of course, Jennifer's life is still often newsworthy, and her newfound attempt to have a quieter existence has not been without problems. For example, in 2006, Jennifer had to get a court injunction to prevent her first husband, Ojani Noa, from publishing a ghost-written tell-all book about their short marriage. The book allegedly stated that Jennifer had cheated on Noa numerous times, including an affair with Marc Anthony while still in her first marriage. Early in 2007, Jennifer and Ojani were ordered by a judge to go into arbitration, or private negotiations, to try to settle the case.

RUMORS

Jennifer's efforts to withdraw somewhat from the limelight have also not stopped rumors about her life from continuing to circulate at high speed. One well-known rumor, which has existed for years, alleges that Jennifer has insured her body for millions of dollars.

Another, more recent rumor claimed she joined the controversial Church of Scientology. This story apparently began because Jennifer is friendly with two famous scientologists, Tom Cruise and Katie Holmes. Adding to the rumor mill is the fact that another close friend, actress Leah Remini, is a member. It has also been reported that Jennifer's father has also converted to the church.

"I'M JUST WORRIED SOMEONE'S GONNA WAKE ME"

Jennifer has always had a lot of confidence in herself and has always worked steadily, so her rise to fame and success has not been a big surprise. What has surprised her sometimes, Jennifer says, is people's expectations. She comments:

> When all the press started happening, I was like: 'My God, what have I done?' It's not exactly something that happened overnight. It feels more like a steady climb. I started out dancing in videos, followed by musical theatre, then moved to television and finally on to movies. I don't think I've changed but there is the aspect that people's perception of you changes when you become famous. . . . Somebody who obviously had faith once told me: 'When you become a star everybody around you is going to say you've changed, but it's not going to be you. What will change is everybody around you, the way they look at you.' I think there's an element of truth in that.*

Jennifer's self-confidence does not seem to have faltered in recent years. She told a reporter that it is connected to the fact that she works hard. "I'll just get better as I go along," she says, "because I'm open to getting better. If you have the goods, there's nothing to be afraid of. If somebody doesn't have

There have also been persistent rumors for years about Jennifer starting a family. Of course, she is now a stepmother to Marc Anthony's three children, but she has never made a secret of her desire to have children of her own. Yet she has also made it clear that she will wait until the proper time. As she told *PEOPLE en Español* magazine, "I come from a strong family, so of course I want to have one. But I do have my own family: my immediate family, my husband and his children. I get to share in all of that. I am very lucky to have that."[93] As for

the goods, they're insecure. I don't have that problem. I'm not the best actress that ever lived, but I know I'm pretty good."**
Jennifer insists, however, that success has not altered her basic personality:

People always ask me, 'Have you changed from what you were?' And I'm always like, 'No way!' And they find it so hard to believe. And I go, 'Look, I'm not saying my life hasn't changed. But I am still the person I started off as.' Has it affected me? Do things get weird? Yes. But I am still Jennifer. I did grow up poor, and I did, you know, wear holey sneakers and hand-me-downs. I did sleep in the bed with my two sisters. And now it's different. It's different because I worked hard to get here. And I never take it for granted. I really do realize, like, oh, my gosh, I wanted to do this my whole life and now I'm able to do it. It feels amazing, you know what I mean? I'm just worried someone's gonna wake me.***

*   Quoted in Martyn Palmer, "Jennifer Lopez Interview." *Total Film*, December 1998.
**   Quoted in Stephen Rebello, "The Wow." *Movieline*, February 1998.
*** Quoted in Mike Sager, "Interview: Jennifer Lopez." *Esquire*, July/August 2003.

the prospect of more kids, elsewhere she has remarked that the question is not for her to answer but up to God.

Enduring years of exposure to nonstop rumors has taught Jennifer how to handle untrue stories about herself. She says she used to get much more disturbed about them than she does now. Now, she says, she lets it slide: "You laugh it off, you get upset for a little while, you're human and you let it go."[94]

"YOU KNOW WHAT I MEAN?"

Despite the disappointments of *Jersey Girl* and *Rebirth*, Jennifer has maintained a steady, and mostly successful, work output in recent years. For instance, the actress dusted off her long-dormant dancing skills in 2004's *Shall We Dance?* In this remake of a hit Japanese film, Jennifer plays an emotionally distant ballroom dance teacher who rekindles a zest for life in a lonely man (played by Richard Gere). *Shall We Dance?* was extremely popular, making the sentimental movie Jennifer's most successful film internationally to date.

The story had a deep meaning for the star. She said at the time of its release: "It's about a woman who doesn't want to deal with her emotions, so she shuts down. And it's such a metaphor for where I am in my life. I just want to keep everybody back and say, 'Hold on, give me some space, let me figure out what all of this means.' I feel like I need to develop a whole new approach because of everything I've been through."[95]

Another outstanding film from this period was *An Unfinished Life,* a modern Western drama released in 2005. It was critically acclaimed, but it did so poorly at the box office that *Forbes* magazine called it "a bona fide flop."[96] In it, Jennifer plays a down-on-her-luck widow and mother who is forced to move to a rundown ranch owned by her gruff father-in-law. There is considerable tension between this woman and the older man (played by Robert Redford), as he blames her for the death of his only son. Jennifer says that her role in *An Unfinished Life* spoke powerfully to her. "Having been hurt by things in my life, I know what it is to pull yourself out of that and to keep going," she says. "I also know how easy it is to let life and the circumstances drag you down and let your life take a course that you never imagined. You know what I mean?"[97]

MONSTER-IN-LAW AND MORE

Jennifer's fee for her next movie, the 2005 comedy *Monster-In-Law*, made history. She was paid $15 million, making her the highest-paid Latin actress in Hollywood history. Unfortunately, *Monster-In-Law* was not a big hit at the box office or with critics. In it, Jennifer appears alongside another screen legend, Jane Fonda, in a story about a woman who finally finds the perfect man, only to find that the man's mother is relentlessly opposed to the union.

In 2007, *Bordertown,* a thriller about a journalist investigating a series of murders near American-owned factories on the Mexico-U.S. border, was released. It costarred Antonio Banderas and reunited Jennifer with director Gregory Nava, who was behind the camera for *Selena* and *Mi Familia/ My Family.*

Also released in 2007 was *El Cantante,* Jennifer's first movie with Marc Anthony. Like *Selena, El Cantante* is a biopic, a film biography. It tells the story of Héctor Lavoe, the Puerto Rican-born entertainer who is called the "King of Salsa." Lavoe, a gifted singer who rose quickly to stardom but was plagued by drug abuse and disease did much to popularize salsa in the 1970s.

VARIETY

Jennifer says she enjoys making a variety of films. Some are high-profile Hollywood movies with big stars, such as *Monster-In-Law* and *An Unfinished Life.* Others are less commercial movies, such as *Bordertown* and *El Cantante,* which make less money but have a more personal meaning for her. The trick, she says, is in balancing the two: "You've got to do your share of commercial movies—romantic comedies, action movies—the $100-million movies, because if you don't you're

The fabulous J.Lo arrives for the screening of her movie, *Bordertown*, during the 57th International Film Festival in Berlin, Germany, in February 2007. Although the film met with poor reviews, Jennifer was honored by Amnesty International for her role as producer and star of the film, which examined the murders of hundreds of women in a Mexican border town.

not going to have the power and Hollywood is not going to respect you. [But] I would also do any small, independent movie that appeals to me dramatically, because it keeps everybody realizing that your acting chops are there."[98]

Jennifer adds that she feels lucky that her success allows her to be choosy in this way. "There was a time in my career when I was offered this, offered that, lots of money, blah, blah, blah! Who cares? Now I feel I'm in a different place where I'm much more picky."[99]

In the end, she says, what matters is the quality of the material. "Great material will win out over anything else," Jennifer remarks. "As an artist, that's what I believe in, it's what I'm passionate about—making good movies and telling good stories."[100]

TELEVISION

Though busy with movies, Jennifer has not neglected occasional TV appearances. For instance, she guest-starred in the sixth-season finale of *Will & Grace* in 2004, playing herself. More recently, Jennifer was a performer and vocal coach on an episode of *American Idol* in April 2007. Jennifer's appearance on *American Idol* received the highest ratings of any of the show's celebrity "mentors," which included Gwen Stefani, Tony Bennett, and Diana Ross. Jennifer coached finalist Sanjaya Malakar to a performance that even the show's famously nasty judge, Simon Cowell, admitted "wasn't terrible."[101] She also spent about 10 minutes face-to-face with other *Idol* contestants. One of these, ninth-place finisher Haley Scarnato, commented, "She was great. She was very warm and comforting, and she had a lot to tell us, and you could tell she really wanted to help us."[102]

A larger commitment to television has been through the production company Jennifer formed, Nuyorican Productions. As a producer, she has the ability to create and control new projects from start to finish, a process that she says is tough but fascinating: "You come up with the idea, decide on a director,

ROLE MODEL WITH
A SOCIAL CONSCIENCE

Everyone who has followed Jennifer's life knows that she has had several high-profile love affairs. These have included her first husband, waiter/model Ojani Noa; rapper/entrepreneur Sean "Puffy" Combs; her second husband, dancer Cris Judd; actor Ben Affleck; and her third husband, singer Marc Anthony.

Each of these men comes from a different ethnic background, and it is apparent that Jennifer does not look at skin color when choosing a romantic partner. In this respect, she can be seen as a role model for people who hope to bring down the barriers between the world's races and ethnic heritages. She comments:

> I don't look at people and see color and race. I see inside. If you look at the people I've been with, there's no type. Ojani was from Cuba—different from me, a Latina born here. Puffy and I grew up in the same kind of background, but he's African American. You have Cris, who was Asian, Filipino. Then there's Ben [who is white, and Marc, who is of Puerto Rican descent].*

Elsewhere, Jennifer has spoken out about how quick some people are to judge others by their skin color or other appearance. "People are so quick to form an opinion of you. . . . They want to figure you out in five minutes, and there's no way you can do that. People take one look at me or judge me on one thing I do and decide what I'm like. I'm not saying it's a good or bad thing, but that's the way it is."**

Jennifer's deep sense of commitment and dedication also serves as a model for young and old alike. In the media, Jennifer's success following *Selena* was often seen as sudden stardom. Yet, Jennifer was *not* an overnight sensation. She had been working hard for years to attain her goal of being a star. She reflects, "When all the press started happening, I was like: 'My God, what have I done?' It's not exactly something that happened overnight. It feels more like a steady climb. I started out dancing in videos, followed by musical theatre, then moved to television and finally on to movies."***

As a performer who can command up to $15 million per film, Jennifer sees her stunning financial success in show business as a vindication for the years of hard work and effort put in by Latino entertainers over the decades. She hopes that those who come after her will benefit from her efforts. As she notes, "I just feel that Latinos have been underpaid in every way long enough. So if it is true [that things are changing], then I'm happy about it. Especially in show business, if I can help further the Latino community in any way, I just feel proud to have the opportunity."†

Yet it is not only the Latino community to which Jennifer makes significant and lasting contributions. Jennifer is involved in many charitable efforts, supporting causes such as at-risk and disadvantaged youth, cancer, health, children, human rights, organ donation, and unemployment/career support. In recent years, Jennifer was particularly busy in her charitable work. Teaming up with husband, Marc Anthony, the couple turned out to support the Children's Health Fund at a 2007 gala fundraiser to promote quality healthcare for all children. At the event, Jennifer commented, "I think it's our responsibility as human beings to do as much as we can to help each other. And for us, for me, I've always had close to my heart the children's charities."††

Earlier in the year, Jennifer received Amnesty International's Artists for Amnesty Award for her role as producer of *Bordertown*, a film exposing the ongoing murders of hundreds of women in the border city of Juarez, Mexico. "It sends a strong message to the public when someone like Jennifer Lopez demonstrates her personal commitment to a cause," said Larry Cox, executive director of Amnesty International USA (AIUSA). "We are thrilled that her support will help us reach entirely

(continues on page 94)

(continued from page 93)

new audiences who can invigorate an international movement to save women's lives."[†††]

[*]   Quoted in Sara Davidson, "Face to Face with Jennifer Lopez: The Little Latina Girl from the Bronx is all Grown Up." *Reader's Digest*, August 2003.

[**]   Quoted in Anthony Noguera, "Latin Lessons: *Out Of Sight* Star Jennifer Lopez Tells FHM the Ways a Man Can Make it Into Her Good Books." *FHM*, December 1998.

[***]   Quoted in Martyn Palmer, "Jennifer Lopez Interview." *Total Film*, December 1998.

[†]   Quoted in Bob Strauss, "Jennifer Lopez's Family Values." *Los Angeles Daily News*, August 13, 1996.

[††]   Quoted in Myrlia Purcell, "Lopez, Marc Anthony, Paul Simon United for Children's Health." Available online. URL: www.looktothestars.org/celebrity/93-jennifer-lopez.

[†††]   Amnesty International, USA, "Jennifer Lopez to Receive Amnesty International's 'Artists for Amnesty' Producing *Bordertown*." Available online. URL: www.amnestyinternational.usa.org.

think about locations, the film stock. It's endless. I get goose bumps."[103]

Her first effort was a short-lived dramatic series called *South Beach*, about the fast-paced world of Miami's night-clubs and models. It was not popular and was cancelled in 2006 after only eight episodes. The series later ran into more problems than just low ratings. A television writer is suing Jennifer and others involved in the series' production, alleging that the idea for *South Beach* was stolen from a show he created in 1999.

Jennifer is also the executive producer of a reality show called *DanceLife*, in which six aspiring dancers try to make it professionally. Besides actively helping to select participants, Jennifer has made cameo appearances during the course of *DanceLife*. The series has been a gratifying hit, as she comments: "The success of *DanceLife* proved to me that I should be much more active as a producer."[104]

AN ALL-SPANISH ALBUM

Meanwhile, Jennifer has not been ignoring her singing career. She released her first all-Spanish album, *Como Ama una Mujer* ("How a Woman Loves"), in 2007. Its first single was "Qué Hiciste" ("What Have You Done"). The album, coproduced by Marc Anthony, had been strongly anticipated by her fans, and Jennifer declared, "To release an album in Spanish was my dream. It was the aim of my career and it is the album I am proudest of."[105]

The singer debuted *Como Ama una Mujer* in the Bronx before hundreds of fans. In Spanish she told them, "I want to say thank you to everyone for coming to celebrate this very special day with me," and in English added, "It touches my heart to be able to bring this album back to my neighborhood, back to my home."[106] Despite the high expectations, the CD sold relatively poorly, racking up fewer than 50,000 copies in its debut week and falling out of the Top 10 in only its second week on the sales charts.

The album's title song inspired a five-hour miniseries produced for a Spanish-language cable network. This is a musical drama about lost love in Hollywood. Jennifer, the series' executive producer, says she thought up the story line while taking a long bath.

Como Ama una Mujer created a controversy shortly after its release. A major Spanish-language music store chain, Ritmo Latino, accused Jennifer's record company of refusing to schedule her to do personal appearances promoting the new album. The company retaliated by banning all of her CDs from its stores. Ritmo Latino's president, David Massey, was upset that his company had supported Jennifer from the beginning of her record career and was now being told that she would only make personal appearances at large Anglo-oriented stores. "This is a Spanish-language CD," he fumed, "and if she wants to discriminate against the Latin community, then we will not sell her product. This is not the first time this has happened. Celebrities have this notion that when they reach a certain level of crossover appeal, they forget quickly where they started. We will no longer tolerate these situations."[107]

MORE PERFORMANCES

Jennifer's next English-language album was released in fall 2007. She collaborated on it with a variety of top-notch producers, including Swizz Beatz, Timbaland, Cory Rooney, and Jermaine Dupri. "It's coming out incredible," according to Swizz Beatz. "We're putting together some great things, and not what everyone's expecting. . . . It's real feel-good music."[108]

Although Jennifer has no plans to stop touring, she has reached a point where she can, and does, make only those live performances that most appeal to her. Some of these can be very lucrative. In April 2007, a Russian banking billionaire paid over $2 million to have Jennifer perform a 40-minute set at a party in honor of his wife's thirtieth birthday. This money included Jennifer's $1.2 million fee, in addition to the $800,000-plus it cost the billionaire to bring the singer, her husband, and their entourage to his estate in England.

CLOTHING AND PERFUMES

In recent years, Jennifer has been engaged in marketing fashion products and related accessories. She has appeared in ads for such companies as luxury leather-goods maker Louis Vuitton and for Lux shampoo in Japan.

Jennifer has also branched out to start her own hugely successful lines of products, following the example of many movie and music stars, including her ex-boyfriend Puffy Combs. Among the clothing lines Jennifer has started are "JLO by Jennifer Lopez," "JustSweet," and "Sweetface." She also

A 10-year-old fan gets a happy hug from Jennifer after the pop star's performance in New York's Rockefeller Plaza during the NBC *Today* show concert series, in March 2005. The youngster got to meet Jennifer, who was out promoting her album *Rebirth*, by winning the Jennifer Lopez "Biggest Littlest Fan" contest sponsored by the show.

markets her own jewelry and a line of accessories such as hats, gloves, and scarves.

Jennifer's line of fragrances have sold extremely well, with combined global sales of more than $500 million. Some published reports estimate that her perfumes and clothing lines, if taken together, earn Jennifer even more than she brings in from her music and movies. Among the perfumes she has created are "Glow by JLo," "Still," and a limited-edition perfume called "Miami Glow by JLo." Newer fragrances include "Live by Jennifer Lopez," "Love at First Glow by JLo," "Live Luxe," and "Glow After Dark." She also markets a "Glow" line of body lotions and bronzers.

MORE FASHION

Jennifer has focused on fashion-related products for several reasons. One, of course, is simply financial. Jennifer knows that she will not always be a top-earning movie or singing star. Public tastes will change, and she will no longer be a bankable commodity. As she puts it, "You work so hard your whole life—it's hot, hot, hot, and then it's cold. I know that day will come. . . . I'm not stupid. I would like to have some businesses that grow so I won't have to be out there on the road when I'm forty-four."[109]

Another reason for Jennifer's focus on fashion is simply that she loves it. She has always gotten a thrill out of wearing the creations of such top-end designers as Valentino, Wang, Prada, and Dolce & Gabbana. She has also always loved shopping, though she admits, "I don't enjoy shopping like I used to."[110]

Jennifer's love of fashion, such as her fondness for fur, has generated its share of controversy. She likes to wear fur, and she likes to include it in many of her clothing designs.

This has led to frequent criticism from animal-rights groups. Such prominent anti-fur activists as Heather Mills McCartney, the former wife of Paul McCartney, have publicly condemned Jennifer. People for the Ethical Treatment of Animals (PETA), a prominent organization devoted to animal rights, has even created an anti-Jennifer Web site, complete with a "Fur Bully from the Block" game, to publicize its disapproval. Anti-fur activists feel so strongly about the issue that Jennifer has allegedly received death threats over the question.

THE FUTURE

What does the future hold for Jennifer Lopez? What will Jennifer do for the next chapters of her life? In a light-hearted mood, she told the German magazine *Bravo* that she has political ambitions. "I'm a total powerhouse," she remarked. "If you ask me, I'd like to become the first female president. That would be really cool. The first thing I would do is redecorate the White House, it doesn't look very cozy."[111]

Until then, Jennifer says, there is much more professionally that she would like to do— more movies, more albums, more opportunities to seize. The actress simply wants to do as much as possible. She comments, "I think I have much more to offer. I would feel bad if I reached the age of sixty and thought about what I should have done."[112]

There are also her personal and professional relationships with Marc Anthony that she tends to. The couple owns several houses, including one in the Bel Air section of Los Angeles, an estate in Old Westbury, Long Island (not far from New York City), and one on Fisher Island near Miami. She and Anthony, Jennifer says, "are a team. He makes me slow down and keeps me grounded."[113]

Jennifer also says that in the future she would like to get rid of her famous nicknames, such as "J.Lo" and "Jenny from the block" because she feels that she is starting to mature. "I'm not J.Lo anymore," she insists. "I'm Jennifer Lopez. I think, as a woman, I've finally grown more sure of who I am."[114]

No matter what she is called, it seems certain that Jennifer Lopez will be an important star—and an important figure in Latino entertainment—for years to come.

Chronology

1969   Jennifer Lynn Lopez born July 24 in the Bronx, NY,
        to David Lopez and Guadalupe Rodriguez.

1987   Appears in the low-budget independent film
        My Little Girl.

        Dances in the musical *Synchronicity* in Japan.

1991   Appears as a Fly Girl dancer on the television show
        In Living Color.

1993   Appears in Janet Jackson's "That's the Way Love Goes"
        video as a backup dancer.

1995   Hits the big screen in *Mi Familia/My Family.*

        Takes David Cruz, sister Lynda, and her mother to the
        Hollywood premiere for the action-comedy *Money Train,*
        in which she costars with Wesley Snipes and Woody
        Harrelson.

1996   Lands the coveted lead role in the movie *Selena.*

1969
Jennifer Lynn
Lopez born in
Bronx, NY

1993
Appears
Janet Jackson
music video
as a backup
dancer

1997
Marries
Ojani Noa
in Miami

1969   1997

1991
Appears as
a Fly Girl
dancer on
*In Living
Color*

1996
Lands coveted
lead role in the
movie *Selena*

Appears in *Jack* with costar Robin Williams and in *Blood and Wine* with Jack Nicholson.

1997   In February, marries Ojani Noa in Miami.

On March 21, *Selena* is released.

Appears in *Anaconda* and *U Turn,* costarring Sean Penn and Nick Nolte.

1998   *Out of Sight* is released, costarring George Clooney.

Appears as the voice of Azteca in *Antz.*

1999   On June 1, debut album, *On the 6*, is released. It produces five hit singles, including "If You Had My Love," and goes triple platinum, selling over three million copies.

On December 27, taken by police with boyfriend Sean "Puffy" Combs after a member of Combs's entourage fires gunshots into the air. Lopez is cleared of charges, and Combs is charged with illegal gun possession and bribery.

1999
Debut album,
On the 6,
is released

2001
Marries Cris Judd; Second studio album, *J.Lo*, debuts at number one

2007
Receives the Artists for Amnesty International award

1999

2007

2000
Appears in "The Dress" at the Grammy Awards

2004
Marries singer Marc Anthony

2000   In January, nominated for two American Music Awards: Pop/Rock New Artist and Favorite Latin Artist.

On February 23, rocks the red carpet and turns heads at the Grammy Awards, appearing in "The Dress," a revealing Versace gown. In September, nominated for a Latin Grammy Award for Best Music video, "No Me Ames" with Marc Anthony.

2001   Tops the box office in romantic comedy *The Wedding Planner*, costarring Matthew McConaughey.

Second studio album, *J.Lo*, debuts at number one, making her the first performer to have the top album and top film simultaneously.

On September 29, marries Cris Judd.

In November, begins production on the comedy *Gigli* where she meets costar Ben Affleck. Jennifer's salary for the movie is $12 million, an increase of $3 million more than her performance in *The Wedding Planner*.

2002   On February 5, *J to tha L-O!: The Remixes* is released, debuting at number one on the charts, the first remix album to accomplish the feat.

In April, opens elegant Cuban restaurant in Pasadena, California, named Madre's.

On July 25, files for divorce from Cris Judd. The romance with Affleck heats up, and in November, he gives Jennifer a pink diamond engagement ring reportedly worth $1.2 million.

In November, wins an MTV Europe Music Award for Best Female.

On November 26, *This Is Me . . . Then* is released, reaching the number-one spot on the charts.

2003   Wins an American Music Award for Favorite Pop/Rock Female Artist.

On August 1, *Gigli* opens to poor reviews. The response from critics forces the postponement of Jennifer's second film with Affleck, *Jersey Girl*.

In October, *J.Lo* is certified for sales of four million copies.

2004   In January, ends romantic relationship with Affleck.

In April, appears on the TV show *Will & Grace*.

On June 5, weds singer Marc Anthony in a private ceremony.

2005   On March 1, the album *Rebirth* debuts. Sales peak at 1.5 million.

In May, *Monster-in-Law*, costarring Jane Fonda, is released.

On December 5, begins filming *El Cantante* with husband, Marc Anthony.

2007   In January, gets top place in *People en Español*'s list of the top 100 Most Influential Hispanics. Her empire that includes movies, music, clothing, and fragrances is estimated at $255 million.

In February, receives the Artists for Amnesty International Award for her work as producer and star of *Bordertown*, a film exposing the murders of women in Juarez, Mexico.

Como Ama una Mujer, first full Spanish-language album is released in March.

El Cantante is released.

Notes

Chapter 1

1 Quoted in "Biography for Jennifer Lopez," Internet Movie Data Base. Available online. URL: http://www.imdb.com/name/nm0000182/bio.

2 Quoted in Kathleen Tracy, *Jennifer Lopez* (London, ECW Press, 2000), p. 11.

3 "Biography for Jennifer Lopez," Internet Movie Data Base.

4 Reuters, "J.Lo tops list of Most Influential Hispanics," *China Daily*, January 5, 2007.

5 Quoted in "Jennifer Lopez Ditches J.Lo.," RealGuide, April 2, 2007. Available online. URL: http://europe.real.com/guide/bang/1/7128.html.

6 Quoted in "No Jennifer Lopez News Today." *The Onion*, March 14, 2001. Available online. URL: http://www.theonion.com/content/node/28660.

7 "Biography for Jennifer Lopez," Internet Movie Data Base.

8 Quoted in Degen Pener, "From Here to Divinity." *Entertainment Weekly*, October 9, 1998.

9 "Biography for Jennifer Lopez," Internet Movie Data Base.

10 Pener, "From Here to Divinity."

Chapter 2

11 Quoted in Sara Davidson, "Face to Face with Jennifer Lopez: The Little Latina Girl From the Bronx is All Grown Up." *Reader's Digest*, August 2003. Reprinted online. URL: http://www.rd.com/content/interview-with-jennifer-lopez/.

12 Ibid.

13 Ibid.

14 Quoted in Anthony Noguera, "Latin Lessons: *Out Of Sight* Star Jennifer Lopez Tells FHM the Ways a Man Can Make it into Her Good Books." *FHM*, December 1998.

15 Ibid.

16 Quoted in Patricia Duncan, *Jennifer Lopez* (New York: St. Martin's Paperbacks, 1999), 4.

17 Ibid., 41.

18 Quoted in Simran Khurana, "J.Lo Quotes." Available online. URL: http://quotations.about.com/od/recentpopularcelebrities/a/jlo_quotes2.htm.

19 Quoted in "About Jennifer Lopez." Available online. URL: http://www.geocities.com/Hollywood/Set/6023/lopeztabla.htm.

20 Quoted in Noguera, "Latin Lessons."

21 Quoted in "Jennifer and Salma Vie for Plum Cleopatra Role." *Mirror* magazine, *Sunday* (Sri Lanka) *Times*, February 11, 2001. Available online. URL: http://lakdiva.org/suntimes/010211/mirrorm.html.

22 Quoted in "IMDB Movie TV News," April 15 2002. Available online. URL: reprinted on http://www.imdb.com/news/wenn/2002-04-15.

23 "Biography for Jennifer Lopez," Internet Movie Data Base.

24 Quoted in Barney Hoskyns, "Selena—Interview with Actress Jennifer Lopez." *Interview*, April 1997.

25 Quoted in Duncan, *Jennifer Lopez*, 5.

26 Quoted in Guy Garcia, "Another Latin Boom, But Different." *New York Times*, June 27, 1999.

Chapter 3

27 Noguera, "Latin Lessons."

28 Duncan, 5.

29 Hoskyns.

30 Duncan, 8.

31 Duncan, 7.

32 Quoted in Joseph Hooper, "J.Lo

Gets Right." *Elle,*
September 2005.
33 Ibid.
34 Hoskyns, "Selena."
35 Tracy, *Jennifer Lopez,* 70.
36 Hooper.

Chapter 4
37 Quoted in Bonnie Siegler,
"(Puff) Daddy's Girl: An
Interview with Actress Jennifer
Lopez." *DrewLive: Celebrity
Stories.* Available online. URL:
http://www.drdrew.com/
DrewLive/article.asp?id=458.
38 Hooper.
39 Hooper.
40 Hoskyns, "Selena."
41 Quoted in "Jennifer Lopez:
Five Fun Facts." People.com.
Available online. URL: reprinted
on http://www.people.com/
people/jennifer_lopez.
42 Duncan, *Jennifer Lopez,* 1-2.
43 Quoted in Bob Strauss, Bob,
"Putting an Icon on Film:
Preserving a Legacy." *Los Angeles
Daily News,* March 16, 1997.
44 Hoskyns, "Selena."
45 Tracy, *Jennifer Lopez,* 82.
46 Quoted in Martha Frankel,
"Jennifer Lopez Loves To . . ."
Cosmopolitan, March 1999.
47 Roger Ebert, "Selena." *Chicago
Sun-Times,* March 21, 1997.
48 Quoted in Tracy, 104.
49 Quoted in Louis B. Hobson,
"Lopez Takes the Heat." *Calgary*
(Alberta) *Sun,* October 5, 1997.
50 Quoted in "Biography for
Jennifer Lopez," Internet Movie
Data Base.
51 Quoted in Tracy, 120.
52 Quoted in David Handleman,
"Jennifer Lopez Can't Be
Stopped." *Mirabella,* July/
August 1998.
53 Ibid.
54 Hooper, "J.Lo Gets Right."
55 Quoted in Tracy, 111.

56 Frankel, "Jennifer Lopez Loves
To . . ."
57 Pener, "From Here To Divinity."
58 Ibid.
59 Quoted in Stephen Rebello,
"The Wow." *Movieline,*
February 1998.
60 Ibid.
61 Ibid.
62 Ibid.
63 Pener, "From Here To Divinity."
64 Quoted in Martyn Palmer,
"Jennifer Lopez Interview." *Total
Film,* December 1998.
65 Tracy, *Jennifer Lopez,* 117.
66 Pener, "From Here To Divinity."

Chapter 5
67 Quoted in Veronica Chambers
and John Leland, "Lovin' La
Vida Loca." *Newsweek,* May 31,
1999.
68 Quoted in Michael A. Gonzales,
"Jennifer's Many Phases." *Latina,*
March 1999.
69 Tracy, 150.
70 Quoted in Elysa Gardner, "She's
All That." *In Style,* June 1999.
71 Gonzales, "Jennifer's Many
Phases."
72 Quoted in David Browne,
"Worst Music." *Entertainment
Weekly,* December 24, 1999.
Available online. URL:
http://www.ew.com/ew/
article/0,,272164,00.html.
73 Quoted in "The Room Service
Waiter is Bemused." *Premiere*
Magazine, August 2000.
74 Quoted in Harriet Ryan, "Driver
Devastates Combs' Defense."
CourtTV, July 18, 2007. Available
online at "CourtTV Online
– Trials." URL: http://www.
courttv.com/trials/puffy/
021501_ctv.html.
75 Tracy, 164.
76 Quoted in "Even Before
Shooting Incident Involving
Boyfriend Sean (Puffy) Combs,

Actress Jennifer Lopez was Told Repeatedly: 'You Can't Be Hollywood's Sweetheart If You're Running From the Cops,' Close Friend Says." *Newsweek,* January 10, 2000. Available online. URL: http://prnwire. com/cgi-bin/stories .pl?ACCT=104&STORY=/ www/story/01-02- 2000/0001106220&EDATE=.

77 "Biography for Jennifer Lopez," Internet Movie Data Base.

78 Quoted in Philip Wuntch, "Even with a Butt-Kicking J-Lo, 'Enough' is enough" *Dallas Morning News,* October 6, 2004. Available online at "Staugustine. com – Archives." URL: http:// www.staugustine.com/ stories/052402/com_731511 .shtml.

79 Quoted in "J.Lo." *SonicNet.* Available online. URL: http:// www.metacritic.com/music/ artists/lopezjennifer/jlo.

80 "J.Lo." *SonicNet.*

81 Quoted in "Jennifer Lopez Makes History Entering The Top 200 Album Chart, The Top R&B/Hip-Hop Album Chart And The Box Office At No.1." *Business Wire,* January 31, 2001.

82 "Biography for Jennifer Lopez," Internet Movie Data Base.

83 Quoted in David Keeps, "It's Hard To Be Me (But It's Good)." *Marie Claire,* September 2004.

84 Quoted in Stephen M. Silverman, "Ben's Proposal 'Beautiful,' Says Lopez." *People,* November 11, 2002.

85 Hooper, "J.Lo Gets Right."

86 Quoted in Chris Booker, "Have J.Lo and Affleck Split?" "IMDB News." Available online. URL: http://www.imdb.com/ name/nm1316432/news.

87 Hooper.

Chapter 6

88 Ibid.

89 Quoted in Kimberley Porteous, "Dancing Queen." Sydney (Australia) *Morning Herald,* October 20, 2004.

90 Quoted in "The Week's Best Celebrity Quotes." People.com, July 18, 2007. Available online. URL: http://www.people.com/ people/gallery/0,,20040428_ 3,00.html.

91 Quoted in Louise Gannon, "Jennifer Lopez is Hotter Than Ever!" *ElleCanada,* April 2007. Available online. URL: http:// www.ellecanada.com/ellecanada/ client/en/Trends/DetailNews. asp?idNews=238536&idSM=441.

92 Quoted in "Jennifer Lopez Says She and Marc Anthony Are a Team." *People,* March 23, 2007. Available online. URL: http://www.people.com/people/ article/0,,20015897,00.html.

93 Quoted in Steven M. Silverman, "Jennifer Lopez Says She Wants Children, 'Of Course.'" *People,* January 4, 2007. Available online. URL: http://www.people.com/ people/article/0,,20006295,00. html.

94 "Biography for Jennifer Lopez," Internet Movie Data Base.

95 Quoted in Keeps, "It's Hard To Be Me."

96 Quoted in Lea Goldman, "Falling Stars." *Forbes,* June 13, 2007. Available online. URL: http://www.forbes.com/ media/2007/06/12/celebrity- superstars-hollywood-cz_lg_ 0612dropoffs.html.

97 Hooper, "J.Lo Gets Right."

98 Rebello, "The Wow."

99 Hooper.

100 Ibid.

101 Quoted in Joal Ryan, "The Jennifer Lopez Effect." E! Online News, Tue, 17 Apr 2007.

Available online. URL:
http://www.eonline.
com/news/article/index.
jsp?uuid=db62a417-a363-
4504-b99d-21e6d65fd0ca.

102 Ibid.

103 Hooper.

104 Quoted in Julio Martinez,
"Jennifer Lopez Partners With
Univison On New Mini-Series."
Latin Heat Online, May 16, 2007.
Available online. URL: http://
www.latinheat.com/
news.php?nid=1151.

105 Quoted in Sureka Fernando,
"Jennifer Lopez Interview."
Cinemas Online, April 2007.
Available online. URL:
http://www.cinemas-online.
co.uk/website/interview.
phtml?uid=145.

106 Quoted in "J.Lo, back on the
block." *USA Today*, March 29,
2007.

107 Quoted in Kerry Burke and
Leo Standora, "J.Lo is Panned
& Banned by Chain." *New York
Daily News*, March 31, 2007.

108 Quoted in "Swizz Beatz

Producing Songs For Britney's
New Album." *BritneySpears.
org.* Available online. URL:
http://britneyspears.hollywood.
com/2006/08/25/swizz-beatz-
producing-songs-for-britneys-
new-album/.

109 Davidson, "Face to Face."

110 Quoted in "Jennifer Lopez
Says She and Marc Anthony
Are a Team."

111 Quoted in "Jennifer Lopez
Wants to be American
President." *ABCNews Online*
(Australia), May 3, 2005.
Available online. URL:
http://www.abc.net.au/news/
newsitems/200505/s1359116.
htm.

112 Duncan, 34.

113 Fernando, "Jennifer Lopez
Interview."

114 Quoted in Louise Gannon,
"You Can't Live at that
Level." *The Guardian*, March
30, 2007. Available online.
URL: http://arts.guardian.
co.uk/filmandmusic/
story/0,,2045396,00.html.

Bibliography

BOOKS

Duncan, Patricia J. *Jennifer Lopez*. New York: St. Martin's Paperbacks, 1999.

Tracy, Kathleen. *Jennifer Lopez*. London: ECW Press, 2000.

NEWSPAPERS, MAGAZINES, WEB SITES, AND WIRE SERVICES

"About Jennifer Lopez." Available online. URL: http://www.geocities.com/Hollywood/Set/6023/lopeztabla.htm.

Amnesty International, USA, "Jennifer Lopez to Receive Amnesty International's 'Artists for Amnesty' Producing *Bordertown*." Available online. URL: www.amnestyinternational.usa.org.

Bardin, Brantley. "1988 Woman of the Year: Jennifer Lopez." *Details,* December 1998.

"Biography for Jennifer Lopez," Internet Movie Data Base. Available online. URL: http://www.imdb.com/name/nm0000182/bio.

Booker, Chris. "Have J.Lo and Affleck Split?" "IMDB News." Available online. URL: http://www.imdb.com/name/nm1316432/news.

Browne, David. "Worst Music." *Entertainment Weekly*, December 24, 1999. Available online. URL: http://www.ew.com/ew/article/0,,272164,00.html.

Burke, Kerry, and Leo Standora. "J.Lo is Panned & Banned by Chain." *New York Daily News,* March 31, 2007.

Chambers, Veronica and John Leland. "Lovin' La Vida Loca." *Newsweek,* May 31, 1999.

Combs, Sean, "Touched by an Angel: Puff Daddy Interviews the Celestial Jennifer Lopez." *Notorious*, October 1999.

Davidson, Sara. "Face to Face with Jennifer Lopez: The Little Latina Girl from the Bronx is All Grown Up." *Reader's Digest,* August 2003. Reprinted online. URL: http://www.rd.com/content/interview-with-jennifer-lopez/.

Ebert, Roger. "Selena." *Chicago Sun-Times,* March 21, 1997.

"Even Before Shooting Incident Involving Boyfriend Sean (Puffy) Combs, Actress Jennifer Lopez was Told Repeatedly: 'You Can't be Hollywood's Sweetheart if You're Running From the Cops,' Close Friend Says." *Newsweek,* January 10, 2000. Available online.

URL: http://prnwire.com/cgi-bin/stories.pl?ACCT=104&STORY=/ www/story/01-02-2000/0001106220&EDATE=.

Fernando, Sureka. "Jennifer Lopez Interview." *Cinemas Online,* April 2007. Available online. URL: http://www.cinemas-online.co.uk/ website/interview.phtml?uid=145.

Frankel, Martha. "Jennifer Lopez Loves To . . ." *Cosmopolitan,* March 1999.

Gannon, Louise. "Jennifer Lopez is Hotter Than Ever!" *ElleCanada,* April 2007. Available online. URL: http://www.ellecanada.com/ ellecanada/client/en/Trends/DetailNews.asp?idNews=238536&idS M=441.

Gannon, Louise. "You Can't Live at that Level." *The Guardian,* March 30, 2007. Available online. URL: http://arts.guardian.co.uk/ filmandmusic/story/0,,2045396,00.html

Garcia, Guy. "Another Latin Boom, But Different." *New York Times,* June 27, 1999.

Goldman, Lea. "Falling Stars." *Forbes,* June 13, 2007. Available online. URL: http://www.forbes.com/media/2007/06/12/celebrity-superstars-hollywood-cz_lg_0612dropoffs.html.

Gonzales, Michael A. "Jennifer's Many Phases." *Latina,* March 1999.

Handleman, David. "Jennifer Lopez Can't Be Stopped." *Mirabella,* July/August 1998.

Hobson, Louis B. "Lopez takes the heat." *Calgary* (Alberta) *Sun,* October 5, 1997.

Hooper, Joseph. "J.Lo Gets Right." *Elle,* September 2005.

Hoskyns, Barney. "Selena—Interview with Actress Jennifer Lopez." *Interview,* April 1997.

"IMDB Movie TV News," April 15 2002. Available online. URL: reprinted on http://www.imdb.com/news/wenn/2002-04-15.

"J.Lo." *SonicNet.* Available online. URL: http://www.metacritic.com/ music/artists/lopezjennifer/jlo.

"Jennifer and Salma Vie for Plum Cleopatra Role." *Mirror* magazine, *Sunday* (Sri Lanka) *Times,* February 11, 2001. Available online. URL: http://lakdiva.org/suntimes/010211/mirrorm.html.

"Jennifer Lopez Ditches J.Lo.," RealGuide, April 2, 2007. Available online. URL: http://europe.real.com/guide/bang/1/7128.html.

"Jennifer Lopez: Five Fun Facts." People.com. Available online. URL: reprinted on http://www.people.com/people/jennifer_lopez.

"Jennifer Lopez Makes History Entering The Top 200 Album Chart, The Top R&B/Hip-Hop Album Chart And The Box Office At No.1." *Business Wire,* January 31, 2001.

"Jennifer Lopez Says She and Marc Anthony Are a Team." *People,* March 23, 2007. Available online. URL: http://www.people.com/people/article/0,,20015897,00.html.

"Jennifer Lopez Wants to be American President." *ABCNews Online* (Australia), May 3, 2005. Available online. URL: http://www.abc.net.au/news/newsitems/200505/s1359116.htm.

Keeps, David. "It's Hard To Be Me (But It's Good)." *Marie Claire,* September 2004.

Khurana, Simran. "J Lo Quotes." Available online. URL: http://quotations.about.com/od/recentpopularcelebrities/a/jlo_quotes2.htm.

Martinez, Julio. "Jennifer Lopez Partners With Univison On New Mini-Series." *Latin Heat Online,* May 16, 2007. Available online. URL: http://www.latinheat.com/news.php?nid=1151.

Noguera, Anthony. "Latin Lessons: *Out Of Sight* Star Jennifer Lopez Tells *FHM* the Ways a Man Can Make it Into Her Good Books." *FHM,* December 1998.

"No Jennifer Lopez News Today." *The Onion,* March 14, 2001. Available online. URL: http://www.theonion.com/content/node/28660.

Palmer, Martyn. "Jennifer Lopez Interview." *Total Film,* December 1998.

Pener, Degen. "From Here to Divinity." *Entertainment Weekly,* October 9, 1998.

Porteous, Kimberley. "Dancing Queen." Sydney (Australia) *Morning Herald,* October 20, 2004.

Purcell, Myrlia. "Lopez, Marc Anthony, Paul Simon United for Children's Health." Available online. URL: www.looktothestars.org/celebrity/93-jennifer-lopez.

Rebello, Stephen. "The Wow." *Movieline,* February 1998.

Reuters, "J.Lo tops list of Most Influential Hispanics," *China Daily,* January 5, 2007.

"The Room Service Waiter is Bemused." *Premiere* Magazine, August 2000.

Ryan, Harriet. "Driver Devastates Combs' Defense." *CourtTV,* July 18, 2007. Available online at "CourtTV Online – Trials." URL: http://www.courttv.com/trials/puffy/021501_ctv.html.

Ryan, Joal. "The Jennifer Lopez Effect." E! Online News, Tue, 17 Apr 2007. Available online. URL: http://www.eonline.com/news/article/index.jsp?uuid=db62a417-a363-4504-b99d-21e6d65fd0ca.

Sager, Mike, "Interview: Jennifer Lopez." *Esquire,* July/August 2003.

Siegler, Bonnie. "(Puff) Daddy's Girl: An Interview With Actress Jennifer Lopez." *DrewLive: Celebrity Stories.* Available online. URL: http://www.drdrew.com/DrewLive/article.asp?id=458.

Silverman, Stephen M. "Ben's Proposal 'Beautiful,' Says Lopez." *People,* November 11, 2002.

Silverman, Stephen M. "Jennifer Lopez Says She Wants Children, 'Of Course.'" *People,* January 4, 2007. Available online. URL: http://www.people.com/people/article/0,,20006295,00.html.

Strauss, Bob. "Putting an Icon on Film: Preserving a Legacy." *Los Angeles Daily News,* March 16, 1997.

"Swizz Beatz Producing Songs For Britney's New Album." *BritneySpears.org.* Available online. URL: http://britneyspears.hollywood.com/2006/08/25/swizz-beatz-producing-songs-for-britneys-new-album/.

"The Week's Best Celebrity Quotes." People.com, July 18, 2007, Available online. URL: http://www.people.com/people/gallery/0,,20040428_3,00.html.

Wuntch, Philip. "Even with a Butt-Kicking J-Lo, 'Enough' is Enough." *Dallas Morning News,* October 6, 2004. Available online at "Staugustine.com – Archives." URL: http://www.staugustine.com/stories/052402/com_731511.shtml.

Further Reading

Hurst, Heidi, *Jennifer Lopez.* Farmington Hills, MI: Lucent, 2004.

Márquez, Herón, *Latin Sensations.* Minneapolis, MN: Lerner, 2001.

Parish, James Robert, *Jennifer Lopez: Actor and Singer.* New York: Ferguson, 2006.

WEB SITES

Jennifer Lopez Official Site
http://www.jenniferlopez.com

Jlo.net
http://www.jlo.net

JLOBronx.com
http://www.jlobronx.com

Picture Credits

page:

Index

About the Author

Adam Woog has written more than 60 books for adults, young adults, and children. He has special interests in biography and music. Woog lives in his hometown, Seattle, Washington, with his wife, Karen, and their daughter, Leah.